Austentatious

Fandom & Culture

Paul Booth and Katherine Larsen, series editors

Austentatious

THE EVOLVING WORLD OF JANE AUSTEN FANS

Holly Luetkenhaus & Zoe Weinstein

UNIVERSITY OF IOWA PRESS · IOWA CITY

University of Iowa Press, Iowa City 52242
Copyright © 2019 by the University of Iowa Press
www.uipress.uiowa.edu
Printed in the United States of America

Text design by Omega Clay

Printed on acid-free paper

Library of Congress Cataloging-in-Publication Data
Names: Luetkenhaus, Holly, 1985– author. | Weinstein,
Zoe, 1990– author.
Title: Austentatious : the evolving world of Jane Austen
fans / Holly Luetkenhaus & Zoe Weinstein.
Description: Iowa City : University of Iowa Press, [2019]
| Series: Fandom & culture | Includes bibliographical
references and index. |
Identifiers: LCCN 2018044858 (print) | LCCN 2018051446
(ebook) | ISBN 978-1-60938-640-5 | ISBN 978-1-60938-639-9
(pbk. : alk. paper)
Subjects: LCSH: Austen, Jane, 1775–1817—Appreciation. |
Austen, Jane, 1775–1817—Influence.
Classification: LCC PR4037 (ebook) | LCC PR4037 .L84 2019
(print) | DDC 823/.7—dc23
LC record available at https://lccn.loc.gov/2018044858

For my husband.

—HOLLY

To my parents, who recorded every Jane Austen adaptation ever on PBS when I was little and who regularly listen to me rant about Austen (or anything else). Thank you for everything.

And to my friends, who pushed and supported me on the phone, skype, in person, at hockey games, and in the gym. Your high-fives, virtual and otherwise, helped me forward.

—ZOE

contents

acknowledgments

First and foremost, Zoe. We somehow managed to balance different time zones, full-time jobs, cross-country moves, and personal crises and still make it to the finish line as not only coauthors, but friends. This book exists because of you.

To my parents, who spent my whole life telling me I could do anything and always pushed me to challenge myself. Mom, you're the strongest woman I know, and I am so blessed to have grown up with you as a parent and role model. Dad, I wish you could be here to see this moment, and to feel the pride you had in me, and in all of your children. And Adam, Alex, Austin, and Aaron, you are the best four brothers a girl could ask for.

To my colleagues, and friends, who kept me motivated and focused, especially Matt and Cristina; working with you and being your friend has brought me more joy and fulfillment than I ever thought a job could offer. I will be forever grateful for whatever plan brought me to Oklahoma, and to your team. Lorena, who "beta'd" sections of my writing and tore it apart so I could make it better.

Finally, to Katherine Larsen, who shared her time and expertise with us as we worked to complete this project.

—HOLLY

Most important, Holly. Thank you for everything. Obvs this book wouldn't exist without you, and I couldn't have asked for a better coauthor and friend.

To my parents, to whom this book is also dedicated. You are amazing and smart and loving. I could not have done this book without your encouragement, read throughs, and your patient listening to all my complaining.

Next, my friends. There are too many to name who helped on this journey. Hannah, Stephanie, Alex, Victoria, Dan, Rey, and Eli are just a few of many, many who helped me, but are especially key to this book existing. Aimee Slater, thank you for listening to me rant about book stuff at work while using your publishing knowledge and helping me not panic. Otavia Propper, thank you for helping me sit my butt down and write, feeding me, and talking me through writing drafts. Piseth Sam, thank you for every ounce of motivation you've instilled in me—without that, this book would be half of what it is.

Next, some industry folks, both fan studies and general academia. To Katherine Larsen, thank you for all of your help, but especially for accepting our first abstract for PCA—without that opportunity we would not be here at all. To Catherine Cocks, thank you for reaching out and getting this project started. To KT Torrey and JSA Lowe, we didn't speak much at PCA 2016, but I've been following you ever since, and you've inspired my academic motivation more than you could know.

Last, a few stray thanks to folks I've mostly never met but who helped a lot along the way: to the McElroys (*The Adventure Zone*, especially), Friends at the Table, *The Great British Bake Off*, and Ngozi Ukazu, who helped me procrastinate. To Brooklyn Boulders Somerville, for providing me with a workspace on occasion, and a place to go and work out my frustration. And, of course, to *The Lizzie Bennet Diaries*, the original inspiration for this whole crazy project; keep telling stories.

—ZOE

From Petticoats to Hashtags

Jane Austen, of course, wise in her neatness, trim in her sedateness;
she never fails, but there are few or none like her.
—Edith Wharton

Another book about Jane Austen? Well, kind of.

The number of books about Austen has long surpassed the number of her original works. Others' pens have dwelt on the author herself, her stories, and the many ways in which people can read and interpret her writings. Our pens are here to celebrate the people who keep reading, watching, and writing: the fans. Here we will explore the fan communities that have sprouted across the internet and investigate the ways in which fans engage with Austen and each other. We examine common tropes among fanworks, the new formats of fan practices, and the themes that emerge across fan platforms.

This text, we hope, will help fans reconnect, or connect for the first time, with fan-made Austen material. In a fandom as old as this, we, the fans and scholars, are all we have left; Austen isn't going to write us any more material. Join us as we dive into big and small pictures of fan-made and fan-opined Austen. Let us, dear reader, explore the intertwining fields of Jane Austen and media and fan studies, as well as the diverse people who make up the contemporary cult of Janeism. Austen can be for everyone, so let's see how everyone does Austen.

When we started this book, we wanted to get an idea of what people associate with Jane Austen. So, naturally, we did a completely unscientific Facebook poll of our friends and family, asking them what they first think of when they hear "Jane Austen." The responses were fairly close to expectations: Petticoats. Manners. Bonnets. Zombies. Colin Firth.[1] Commenters ranged from scholars to pleasure readers; they even included responses from people who have never picked up an Austen novel and only know her stories or name from pop culture or various adaptations. Austen and her works mean different things to different people, and every Austen fan has a story of how they first came to read a novel or see a film, and what keeps them coming back to her and her stories. The depth of her novels—whether they are read as comedies of manners, romances, social commentaries, or any other genre—appeals to diverse groups of readers. Among fans there is never going to be an agreement on which novel is best, which heroine most dear, or which hero most appealing because the experience of reading Austen's novels is so *personal*. The good news is that we live in a time when people can easily share their experiences with other fans, and we can debate and squeal over her books endlessly. Prior to the proliferation of online spaces, fans would have had to travel to meet and interact with other fans, doing such things as visiting Austen-related sites in the UK, traveling to conventions, or joining societies or book clubs. Fans still do this, of course, and new sites have been added to the rotation, such as the Folger Shakespeare Library, where the *actual shirt* Colin Firth wore in the 1995 adaptation was housed. But new media formats, along with the availability of online platforms for fan expressions, mean that fan experiences today have taken on a much more varied and involved state, especially when devotees interact with each other as well as the texts themselves.

Fandom in today's world is as much a community experience as a deeply personal one. Early fans and scholars (we'll get to that combination in a second) interacted with each other through societies, reading groups, letter writing, cons, and zines; the internet has allowed for easier, faster, and cheaper communication. We, the authors of this book, are fans ourselves and experienced different ways of participating in various fandoms online, as well as being Jane Austen fans. There is often a tension that exists between scholarship and fannishness,[2] and it is one that we will touch on as we go through this exploration, since we are both fans and scholars and approach Austen in combination. We identify ourselves as fans because it is our hobby—it's a self-identification. We are scholars because we are paid to be scholars, most of the time. Of course, independent scholars don't always get paid, and scholars in general sometimes aren't paid enough (shout out to our adjunct colleagues), but more often than not it's part of our job. Fandom, though, is something we choose to do in our free time, something we dedicate ourselves to for fun, not profit (though this precludes the idea that fandom practices cannot be done for profit, which is another point of tension among fans themselves, and something we address in this book).[3] So we separate the two, even though both are driven by love of a thing: love of a story or a field of study or a piece of media. In Henry Jenkins's blog series "Acafandom and Beyond," Erica Rand recalls that she was "at a workshop on teaching first year seminars and the person leading it did the icebreaker of having us discuss in small groups an incident in college where we first identified as scholars."[4] It's an interesting anecdote because it rings so true. We were both fans long, long before we pursued scholarly research. Zoe was a fan of *Star Trek* before she could read a novel, and long before she knew what literary criticism was, she was a fan of *Harry Potter* and *Discworld* and *Lord of the Rings*. Holly spent hours obsessing over *Buffy the Vampire Slayer* as a teenager and collecting Jane Austen–related books, watching film adaptations, and dreaming of attending a Regency ball before it ever occurred to her that she might turn her fannish love into scholarly pursuits. Many of us academics were fans first, and it shaped our scholarship significantly. After all, what is scholarship, truly, but fandom put into structure and approved by others? The idea that these two areas easily overlap, though, is still fairly new to fan studies. Henry Jenkins notes that there are different "generations" of scholars operating within fandom, and the first one emphasized the importance of remaining "outside what they were writing about" and "free of any direct implication in their subject matter."[5] We fit into Jenkins's current generation: a group of scholars for whom their fannish identity is not separate and who do not feel the need to maintain a distance from the thing they study.

This is not to say that this tension is completely gone. One important thing about mixing these two worlds is that they operate with seemingly contradicting structures. Fandom does not ask for approval from outside itself: it is by the fans, for the fans, and with few exceptions, anything goes. But scholarship requires an outside mediator and authority. Take this book, for example. We could have written this for *only the fans*, and written whatever we wanted. But because we also want this book to be recognized outside Austen fandom, we have to meet obligations of others: the press, the editors, the scholars in Austen and fan studies. Other people have to approve of the work that we're doing, something that we would not need—nor would we seek it—if this was solely a work of fannishness. Austen fandom in particular has felt these tensions throughout its long history.

Since there have been Jane Austen fans, there has been disagreement over who the "real" Jane Austen is. Fans and scholars alike want to claim her for themselves, leading to various personas being presented and popular throughout history. There is dear, quiet, unassuming Aunt Jane and Jane Austen the revolutionary, the Austen of home theatricals and the Austen of Hollywood films.[6] Her novels were adapted by fans at home to stage theatricals (similar to the fraught staging of "Lovers Vows" in *Mansfield Park*) and assigned in schools before they breached the hallowed halls of universities.[7] It is important to note that her popularity in pop culture was largely driven by women; her place in the literary canon was predominantly pushed by men. So, while the tension between academics and fans has always been present in Austen fan circles, that tension has been further complicated by the fact that there is not a "real" Austen to claim (she is too many things to too many people) and that there is a gender divide among fans and scholars. Devoney Looser, one of today's most well-known Austen scholars and a self-identified fan, and who roller-derbies under the moniker "Stone Cold Jane Austen," notes that Austen's dual legacies of being both scholarly and popular have coexisted for such a long time that "Pop-Austen" cannot "ruin" her place in scholarship.[8] Austen's legacy has always been both scholarly and fannish.

Jenkins's term "aca-fan" (sometimes used without the hyphen) is an important one that we will touch on occasionally in this book, but we think it's important to emphasize that we want to talk about Jane Austen for everyone, scholar and fan, casual observer and dedicated reader. We are both fans and scholars, and for us there isn't a gulf between the two. We loved Austen before we wrote about her and on her. Our scholarship allows us to investigate Austen and Austenites in a manner approved of by other scholars, but we've been investigating Austen for years before that.

Because of this, we'd like to introduce you to us, our fan histories, and our Austen experiences as "Janeites."[9]

Hello. My name is Holly, and I am a Janeite.

What started as a leisurely enjoyment of *Pride and Prejudice* as a teen has morphed into a not-quite obsession and an Austen-related Twitter handle. (My middle name is Jane, so I was obviously meant to use @hollyjaneite for my social media.)

My initiation into Jane Austen and my entry into online fan communities began in two very distinct ways. I was sixteen when I first picked up *Pride and Prejudice*. I was a hopeless reader who was not content with the assigned readings alone, and my English teacher handed me a list of classics to read. I quickly devoured *Pride and Prejudice* and moved on to *Sense and Sensibility* and *Mansfield Park*. I read and reread *Pride and Prejudice* for years, content with Mr. Darcy and Elizabeth's romance and biting wit. It wasn't until the summer between my freshman and sophomore year of college (2004), when I took an independent study, that I finally read her remaining completed novels. These early experiences with Austen were undertaken mostly in isolation or as academic pursuits. None of my friends were reading such old, stuffy books; internet fandom had not quite reached my radar. I read Austen's novels, wrote research papers and discussed her with my professors, and watched the iconic film adaptations, but she existed mainly on my bookshelf and in my head. Fanfiction was not a term I knew; the thought of going online or to conventions and meeting other fans never occurred to me. My Austen fandom, for many years, did not encompass any more than me and my steadily increasing library of Austen-related print and media.

Then came my entry into being a fan on the internet. My first dip into internet fandom actually began with *Buffy the Vampire Slayer*. It was through a basic Google search for "Buffy and Spike" that I found my first-ever work of fanfiction.[10] And it was *steamy*.[11] Through this first encounter, I learned about the fan practice of combining character names (Buffy + Spike = Spuffy), found out that fanfiction existed, and then discovered other fan practices, like fan videos on YouTube. And even though this introduced me to much of the early internet fan practices, my participation in those spaces was still largely isolated. I did not leave comments, make videos, or message other users. I was a lurker and consumer, but not a participant.

Cue *Twilight* and the collective internet losing its mind.

These days I tend to repress (read: deny) how much *Twilight* consumed me upon its initial publication. I was caught up in the zeal along with many of my friends—it became my first experience with a shared "fandom," both in person and online. My friends and I would reread the novels, swoon over Edward and Bella, and scour the internet for fan sites. It was through the *Twilight* fandom that I found even more fan practices, like fanart and discussion forums; was introduced to the terms "fancasting" and "shipping wars";[12] and realized just how deeply involved internet fandom could be. Though I never became so immersed in the fan life to participate in role playing or pilgrimages to Forks, Washington, I cannot deny that I may have dabbled in fanfiction writing. It was an entirely new experience—having this community of complete strangers to talk with about the books and characters, to not be afraid of feeling judged for my excitement over the next book release. My foray into *Twilight* fandom eventually led me into other fan communities, and I was able to reconnect with Austen's works and explore her worlds through avenues I had previously not even known existed. My renewed interest in Austen carried me through an English graduate program and then settled into a rewarding, nonscholarly enjoyment of Austen as a passionate fan. I still reread her books from time to time or rewatch films, follow Austen-related fan blogs on Tumblr or Twitter, and have been known to host the occasional oogle-at-Colin-Firth-in-breeches viewing with friends and fellow Janeites.

My renewed scholarly interest in Austen was sparked by the run of the YouTube series, *The Lizzie Bennet Diaries*, produced by Pemberley Digital, which Zoe actually brought to my attention. Not only could I watch a funny, relatable, modern-day adaptation of *Pride and Prejudice*, but the production introduced me to the use of transmedia[13] in storytelling. Gone were the days of the "choose your own adventure" Austen novel; now I could participate in an ongoing narrative with other fans by tweeting at the characters, following Jane Bennet's fashion blog, and submitting questions that might be addressed during a Q&A video by the characters themselves. When a new episode would release, we would text each other reactions, "fangirling" over what happened that week. When we'd get together, we would discuss not only what happened but how we thought the producers might handle plot points we knew were coming up. Through my own experience of being part of this micro-cosm of Austen fandom, I became interested in the fans themselves: Why are we participating in a story, pretending we don't know how it's going to end? What keeps bringing people back to Austen? What other ways are fans using new media to connect with Austen and each other that I never knew existed? And how are today's fans recreating characters and worlds to fit today's ideals of feminism, romance, and society? Luckily for me, my friend and fellow Austen-lover had the same, and interestingly different, questions.

Zoe: Growing up with Harry Potter and Captain Picard.

My introduction to fandom came with my introduction to *Star Trek*. I don't actually remember how old I was, but my dad and I used to watch *Star Trek*—any version—on TV every week (my captain is Captain Picard but my show and ensemble will forever be *Deep Space Nine*). At a very young age I identified a blazer/shirt combination of my mother's as Star Trek uniform colors and forever called it her "*Star Trek* outfit." It took me a long time to realize that I was . . . well . . . a Trekkie (there's a lot of connotation in that word), but I knew what being a fan was starting at a very young age. So when *Harry Potter* entered my life I knew what it was to be a fan, and I dove in headfirst.

I began reading the series not long after it was released in the United States (Harry was eleven, I was eight), and every summer I waited on tenterhooks for the next installment. Lucky for me, so did most of the internet. During the interminable hiatus between *Goblet of Fire* (2000) and *Order of the Phoenix* (2003), I turned to the World Wide Web to fill the hole that Harry's absence left in my life. According to my mother, in those three years I read nothing other than *Harry Potter*, but in truth I *was* reading a few other things. I did discover fiction-alley.org (est. 2001), and I read fanfiction there regularly. I also read *Quidditch through the Ages* and *Fantastic Beasts and Where to Find Them* and every single post on Mugglenet.com.

Okay, so it *was* mostly *Harry Potter*, both fan-created and official.

But in 2002, in seventh grade, I tested "high" on my "Accelerated Reader" exams and was assigned a college-level reading list that included *Jane Eyre*, *Wuthering Heights*, *Ivanhoe*, and *Roots*. *Pride and Prejudice* was on the list, too, and after reading it I thought it was fine. But *Sense and Sensibility* was listed under "other works by Jane Austen" inside the front cover, and to me *Sense and Sensibility* was *better*. Over the next few years I sought out the rest of Austen's works and enjoyed them all (except *Emma*—although I did read it), and spent long afternoons arguing with a friend about which heroine was better and which was more annoying. But Austen fandom writ large was hard to find, and because my love stemmed from a school assignment and blossomed from there, I didn't feel like it was the same as my other fandoms. I was a fan, sure, but it felt different. My outwardly displayed fandoms stayed centered on Terry Pratchett, *Lord of the Rings*, *Star Trek*, and *Harry Potter*. I had friends who were *LOTR* fans, friends who were *Harry Potter* fans, friends who would do movie marathons of *Star Trek: Generations* and *Star Trek: First Contact* and argue about who the best captain was, what Hogwarts house we all were, which *Discworld* book to get others to read first. . . . This all remained the same, more or less, until graduate school—with one exception.

In college, my very first semester (fall 2008), I had a moment of Austen rediscovery that has shaped my Austen fandom and scholarship since. I had the good fortune of taking a class on gothic literature, and we read the highlights of gothic lit—*Castle of Otranto* through *Frankenstein*—and then we doubled back to read *Northanger Abbey*. I had known Austen was funny, but suddenly, halfway through rereading *Northanger* for the first time in years, I understood. Austen was just like Terry Pratchett—she was a satirist in her own way. Over the course of the next few years, in between my studies of Victorian novels and early modern European history, I reread Austen with a new lens. But I still didn't know many Austen fans who weren't scholars, and so Austen continued to be a scholarly fandom for me. A fun scholarly fandom, certainly, with film/TV adaptations aplenty and much talk of Colin Firth's shirt and Matthew MacFayden's open collar.

It wasn't until graduate school that I found other self-described nerds who were also fans of media I had never thought of as fan-related, like Austen's books. After all, adaptations of a dripping-wet Mr. Darcy aside, Austen's oeuvre had been a mostly academic experience. Suddenly, with the release of *The Lizzie Bennet Diaries* (Pemberley Digital, YouTube) friends, old and new, wanted to talk Austen; I was among fellow Janeites, and boy did I spread the gospel. High school friends, college friends, my coauthor—I encouraged everyone who mentioned YouTube *or* literature to take a look. Yet within online fandom, I continued to lurk, choosing not to participate actively in Austen fandom on Twitter or Tumblr.[14] I had my people that I could (and did) call and text to shout and cry at and with. But I had questions. How had people never read *Pride and Prejudice?* Could I convince people to watch all six hours of the BBC *Pride and Prejudice* with me? Were people faking their ignorance to interact with *The Lizzie Bennet Diaries?* If they were, how did that affect the story? Could this kind of adaptation be done again? Why in the world was the fandom so mean to Lydia? And I got lucky; I found someone who could not answer any of these questions, and instead multiplied them exponentially, but who also changed my view of Austen from scholar to fan and who was also willing to text me excitedly when a statue of a dripping wet Mr. Darcy was announced and when Mr. Darcy's actual formerly wet shirt was to come on tour to the United States. We were *fans*, and we were fans *together.*

Dear Jane

Now that you know a bit more about us and our approach to this book, both as fans and as scholars, we should talk about Jane Austen. She is as much a part of today's pop culture as the Kardashians or the Simpsons, as much in the zeitgeist as Sherlock Holmes or Batman. From a YouTube series to a silver-screen zombie mashup,[15] from full-length immersive novels to Twitter accounts, from MMORPGs[16] to board and card games, there likely is not a piece of modern entertainment or media that hasn't somehow been Austenized. And in the world of social media and fast-paced communication, Austen fans are continually reviving old or finding new ways to interact with each other, the texts, and everyone's dear Jane.

Austen fandom can be traced back to the time of the writer herself, but many credit the publication of *A Memoir of Jane Austen* by James Edward Austen-Leigh as the defining moment for Austenmania. Published in 1870, it sparked an interest in Austen and her works that has held ever since.[17] In this memoir, Austen-Leigh presents a vision of his Aunt Jane as an adoring, modest, serene person, who wrote only for personal enrichment, choosing to gloss over stories of her dislike of children, long-standing disagreement with her mother, and desire to publish and sell her work.[18] This image of the gentle, sweet aunt has persisted in many other biographical presentations of Austen and contributed to her initial popularity among the first Janeites, who loved Austen's novels for their simple, domestic stories about quaint life in an English town.[19] In more recent memory, scholars and fans can point to the rash of Austen-related adaptations in the 1990s as the impetus for contemporary Austen obsession (the 1995 *Pride and Prejudice* being the highlight of these). Many parts of the nineties Austenmania have crossed over from the fanon[20] into accepted canon, such as Colin Firth as Mr. Darcy in Andrew Davies's 1995 BBC miniseries. Firth's portrayal of the handsome, brooding, arrogant Darcy is so ubiquitous in fan culture, and both Firth and his swim in a pond are now such an accepted part of Austen canon, that many contemporary adaptations and spin-offs refer to the portrayal. Take, for example, the miniseries *Lost in Austen*, where Amanda, who travels back in time to the story of *Pride and Prejudice* and assumes the role of Elizabeth, asks Elliot Cowan's Mr. Darcy to take a dive in a Pemberley pond as an homage to Firth's now iconic scene. Winks are also thrown to Firth's Darcy in everything from *The Lizzie Bennet Diaries* to Helen Fielding's *Bridget Jones's Diary*[21] to other actors' charity photoshoots.[22] Austen fannishness is now so widespread (and commercialized) that the lines between canon and fanon are blurred considerably. But we should pause before we jump to the present day—there is a long history of Austen fans between the 1800s and the 1990s.

In *Jane Austen Cults and Cultures*, Claudia Johnson notes that fans of Austen began pilgrimages to various Austen-related sites as early as the 1850s[23] and the first work of Austen fanfiction[24] appeared in 1914, entitled *Old Friends and New Fancies* by Sybil G. Brinton and even included non-canon pairings of characters.[25] Austen's completed novels were often given to soldiers in war-torn Europe during the First World War; they were, due to their idyllic settings and structured stories, even prescribed for shell-shocked soldiers after the war ended, to be used for PTSD treatments.[26] As time went on, though, with the creation of Austen societies and the canonization of her literature into high school curricula, the majority of fans moved toward academia.

Two of the most well-known groups for Austen enthusiasts are the Jane Austen Society (JAS) and the Jane Austen Society of North America (JASNA), founded in 1940 and 1979, respectively. JAS is based in the UK, and was originally formed to help preserve and maintain the residence where Austen lived with her mother and sister in Chawton; the purpose of the society has since expanded to include events, newsletters, regional branches, and various publications.[27] The other, JASNA, is based in the US, and like its counterpart, hosts national events, regional gatherings, publications, and even a scholarship contest (and, importantly, a Regency ball on the final day of their national conference).[28] Both societies invite anyone who loves Austen or her works to join and attend events, not restricting participation to any particular group. A video, filmed in 2015 at the JASNA Annual General Meeting (AGM), features a wide range of Austen fans sharing how they first encountered—and kept coming back to—Jane. Those featured in the film represent how truly varied Austen fans are: they are young and old, and men and women; they range from university professors to farmers to scientists and all have a unique story of their relationship to Austen and her works.[29] Societies like JAS and JASNA have been offering a space for devotees to gather and immerse themselves in all things Austen long before the internet made it incredibly easy and cheap to meet and interact with other fans. The internet has also provided space for fans to create their own spaces that are not tied to an official organization. Many of these online fan communities have grown around fanfiction and have their own rules, priorities, and formats.[30]

Being an Austen fan, being a Janeite, is certainly nothing new, and not restricted to present-day fans. Her novels have perhaps been loved at different times for different reasons, but since their publication they have sparked a fan base as rabid as that for Sherlock Holmes.[31] Modern-day fans, however, have found ever-evolving ways to enjoy the novels, interact with each other, and pay homage to the author and her characters. With the rise of the internet and the pervasiveness of social platforms, fan participation has changed considerably from early Austen pilgrimages. While many fans still desire to visit Austen-related sites in the UK (and devotees still flock to those sites every year), the internet has allowed for the creation of more spaces for fans and the ability for fans, many of whom may not have the means or desire to travel to an Austen-related destination or society meeting, to still be active and engaged in a fandom. Recent years have also seen the introduction of even more new forms of media through which Austen can be reimagined and enjoyed.

And so we return to the problem of scholar vs. fan. Austen scholars en-gage in "fan activity" as fans while at academic conferences such as the JASNA annual meeting; during the rather well-known ball during the conference attendees (scholars—and fans) dress up in their best Regency gowns, home-made and professionally tailored alike, to drink and dance and socialize. Cos-play, in other words. Scholars flock to Austen's writing desk to observe the very place where she wrote her famous works. They take pictures of them-selves and enjoy being close to the seat of the true writings, just as any fan does on a fan pilgrimage. We couch fannishness in scholarship to make sure that we aren't coded as "different than" or "other," but we're just fans by any other name. Unfortunately, that coding is present in academia. Melanie Rachel notes in a guest post to the blog Austen Authors that "this kind of frac-tious camp-building isn't limited to Jane Austen. I've seen this kind of divide at least since my own graduate school days, where literature students turned up their noses at MFA students, devaluing the creative and championing the analytical."[32] But it's also present in fandom; fans separate themselves from the "other" all the time, as Mel Stanfill found.[33] There's always someone who is less than you in knowledge or who is "too" into something, whereas you're a reasonable person. They're all stereotypes, and they don't just separate academics from fans but academics from other academics and fans from oth-er fans.

Because of this consistent divide—within fandom, within academia, and between the two—we are going to take an unusual definition of fandom in this book. We are going to define fans, and fandom, as including scholars, professionally published works and authors, and even the BBC and major film productions. Because just as we wouldn't be writing this book if we weren't fans of Austen, the author of Lost in Austen's screenplay, or Andrew Davies, au-thor of the famous 1995 BBC Pride and Prejudice adaptation, wouldn't have put pen to paper or finger to keyboard if they didn't have some love or admiration for Austen or her characters, even if that love is directly tied to her commer-cial appeal. All fans react to other fans differently, but we're all fans. We'll keep saying it because it continues to hold true: Jane Austen is for everyone, so we are here to see how everyone loves Jane Austen.

Austen fandom has cropped up in all forms of media over the last eighty years, from film to Twitter. Many of the Austen film adaptations are well known, but there are perhaps more than people know of: the BBC began with the first (of *Pride and Prejudice*, naturally), released in 1938.[34] Since then, at least one new Austen screen adaptation has appeared in every decade, culminating most recently in *Love and Friendship* (2016), based on Austen's possibly unfinished novella *Lady Susan*, which she later prepped for publication in 1805 and which was published posthumously.[35] The last two decades, however, have seen the most saturated market ever. In the 1990s six screen adaptations based directly on Austen novels were released; in the 2000s there were seven.[36] Those numbers are even higher if you include looser adaptations, like *Clueless* (1995) and *Bridget Jones's Diary* (2001) and the newer adaptations popping up on YouTube. For decades now it has been impossible to escape Jane and her novels, especially on the small screen. And though films and TV adaptations, based heavily or loosely on the novels, continue to be made, Janeite culture has expanded to encompass new media formats as well, such as the transmedia series *The Lizzie Bennet Diaries* and *Emma Approved*, both produced by Pemberley Digital. These series were released as twice-weekly, short YouTube videos, and they incorporated Twitter, blogs, and viewer comments and questions into the narratives. While choose-your-own-adventure–style novels, which allowed fans to immerse themselves in the "Regency experience," had already been around for years, the transmedia focus of these two adaptations showcased a new, twenty-first-century way to interact with the stories, characters, and fans. In addition, fans can also participate in an Austen MMORPG,[37] or converse and share online through message boards, memes,[38] and Tumblr hashtags.[39] The expansion into online and new media formats continues to grow and change, but that has not dulled the fervor in other, more established areas; novels and fanfiction continue to be dominant forces in Austen fandom.

As mentioned previously, the first known work of Austen fanfiction was published in 1914. Written by Sybil Brinton and titled *Old Friends and New Fancies: An Imaginary Sequel to the Novels of Jane Austen*, it reimagined Austen's characters as all existing in one intertwined narrative. The author incorporates primary and secondary characters from all of Austen's major novels, giving those denied a satisfactory ending a chance at their own happily-ever-after. In this reimagined world, the characters of different novels know and visit each other, and Brinton gives subtle, and not-so-subtle, nods to scenes from many of Austen's novels, including a game of charades at Pemberley in reference to *Mansfield's Park*'s similar scene, and Kitty Bennet falling sick after experiencing unrequited love just as Marianne Dashwood does in *Sense and Sensibility*. These little references (sometimes called "easter eggs") are often recognizable only to fans and are an extremely common marker of fanfiction. They are often a signal to other fans that the author is clued in to the pulse of the fandom and is a measuring stick by which one can judge how "in" a reader is, as well.

Fans of Austen have been around a long time, and as evidenced by the early publication of *Old Friends and New Fancies*, the commercialization of Austen fandom has been part of that experience, too. In many fandoms, a written work by a fan might only be able to be called "fanfiction" if it is a (well-loved) hobby, rather than a paid publication.[40] With newer fandoms, copyright laws complicate fan publications as well, as writers and/or artists sometimes have to receive permission (and often pay royalties) for the use of characters or risk lawsuits.[41] But with Austen, whose works have long been in the public domain, there is little to hinder the appeal of continuing to produce, publish, and disseminate Austen-related works for profit, so "fanfiction," for example, can much more easily become a published "reimagining" or "continuation" novel. Austen fans seems to constantly be thirsting for more—for any and all—things that allow them to hold on to Jane just a little bit longer. And today's fans have significantly more outlets for their fervor than fans a hundred years ago.

Austen Fans Online

In this book, we explore fans—scholarly and academic, amateur and professional—of Austen and their interaction with each other and Austen's texts as well as adaptations or spinoffs, with a specific focus on online communities, new forms of media, and transmedia participatory environments. While participation in the Austen fandom is not new, the internet and its ability to reach more people than ever before has helped make it easier to examine what fans are doing, thinking, and sharing. As with any long-standing fandom, the ways readers and fans react and interact with their favorite stories and characters changes as time progresses and societal and cultural norms shift and grow.

After each topical chapter in this book you'll find a case study chapter about one of the themes and how it connects with one of our favorite Jane Austen adaptations. In our first chapter we will talk through how fans create their own stories out of canon, and how that can be hindered and helped by different aspects of a piece of canon text. Fans can be challenged by unclear boundaries and descriptions of a world, such as what happened with the second Austen adaptation by the company Pemberley Digital. *Emma Approved* ran into issues of in- and out-world distinctions, creating a barrier for fans. We also talk through the challenge of creating fan canon (fanon) out of a single actor and how that affects future adaptations and even the understanding of canon itself, and we close the chapter by talking through some of our favorite memes from the past few years and the metatextuality of Austen memes. We follow this with chapter 2, about the adaptation *Clueless* as an example of one of the only truly accurate Austen adaptations in terms of irony. It reflects the feminism of Emma/Cher's actions, and it does so through a character about whom Austen commented that she was sure only she herself would like.

Continuing in the theme of fanon, chapter 3 explores the tangled world of Austen fanfiction, focusing on three major aspects: professionally published works, amateur works, and fanfiction of fanfiction. Within the world of professionally published works, we discuss how the amount of material published and the amount of time since the canon material was published affects how readers today see professionally published fanfictions. For amateur works, we examine general fandom fanfiction sites such as Archive Of Our Own (Ao3) and Fanfiction.net. Last, we discuss the recent blossoming of derivative works with their own fanfiction communities, including the Pemberley Digital productions and *Pride and Prejudice and Zombies*. We examine all of these avenues of fanfiction through a feminist lens, as well as how fanfic writers today carry on Austen's feminist legacy.

Following the themes of feminism in fanfiction, we take a look at a YouTube adaptation in chapter 4 and examine how *The Lizzie Bennet Diaries* translated the social and feminist issues of the 1810s into the 2010s . The adaptation uses smart modernization, and it offers a modernization of Lydia that can preserve the spirit of the story without throwing Lydia out or making her less than her sisters.

The next theme we approach is the issue of representation in the modern Austen fandom. As intersectional studies and fandom studies have come together in the past few years, diversity within fandom and within a text have both become increasingly important. In chapter 5 we discuss casting choices by the company Pemberley Digital and what it means to have Austen characters portrayed by nonwhite actors. We also consider diverse fancasts, head canons, and fanfics, as well as focusing on the representation—or lack thereof—in the Austen fan community online. We focus on the fact that although updated versions of Austen cast diverse actors, or include LGBTQ+ diversity, fandom acts as a separate entity and can create—or not create—a diverse world of its own. Following this examination of representation, in chapter 6 we take a look at how each Austen adaptation brings something new to the table and gives audiences a chance to reflect on how she has changed us in subtle ways. In this case, *Pride and Prejudice and Zombies* souped up Austen's feminism and made it easier for modern audiences to relate to by capitalizing on the trend of genre mashups and zombie stories of the mid-2010s.

Chapter 7 tackles a topic Austen herself was supposed to have never broached: sex, identity, and sexuality. This chapter covers some of the queer subtext in Austen as pointed out by fans, ranging from lesbian romances of Emma and Harriet or Elizabeth and Charlotte to issues of queer representation gone wrong. Luckily, we have examples of queer representation done so, so right, and we talk through the importance of highlighting the queer subtext in classic literature such as Austen and how it can bring in new fans. And for the fans more interested in sex than identity, we discover a world of sex-insert fanfiction and how the language of sex may not blend as well with Austen's ironic style as it would in a typical romance. And yes, we have some . . . spicy examples.

Our last adaptation examination pulls on the themes from chapter 7, and in chapter 8 we take a look at *Love and Friendship* and how it provides a great example of ways for fans (Zoe, in this case) to find queer relationships in traditionally heterosexual media.

In our conclusion, we look inward. We are fans, and we have taken this journey with all of you. But we had to investigate something that we hold incredibly dear. How does that change our view of Austen? Of fandom? Of ourselves? We talk about what's next for our Austen fandom and what we hope to see moving forward as we move through an increasingly connected fandom experience.

We hope that this book will help new fans of Austen discover something old and old fans of Austen discover something new. Our ever-widening definition of fans and fandom means that we hope academics, casual fans, die-hard fans, and everyone in between will find something of use in our examination of modern Austen fandom. We know that there is a perceived gulf between academics and fans, but with a fandom over two hundred years old, with a fandom that began with both academic work *and* "fannish behavior," we hope that readers will put aside their notions of who is a "proper" Austen fan or scholar and simply enjoy the fact that we are all here because we love Austen and her works. We hope that you, dear reader, enjoy this book and that you continue to enjoy Austen, in any form.

1

Fan Canon, Memes, and Mr. Darcy's Wet Shirt

ZOE

Dear Mr Darcy we don't mean to be curt, but we only want to see you in a wet, white shirt.
—Sense and Spontaneity, "Dear Mr Darcy," YouTube

Fans want to be involved. They attend cons, do cosplay, write fanfiction—they seek out more of the story even when there is no more official story out there. So much of fan interaction is the creation of material: from theories (scholarship) to costumes (cosplay) to art (changing medium). When fans come together, they create a new type of community with its own rules and that creates its own content. Sometimes these communities are run by Big Name Fans (BNFs),[1] and sometimes these communities have existed for so long that there are really hundreds of small communities that coexist within the larger space. For Austen, the latter is true while encompassing the former; after all, there have been fans of Austen and her work since there were works to be fans of, and after over two hundred years, the introduction of libraries, mass-produced books and printing houses, radio, movies, television, and the internet, there are hundreds of ways to interact with Austen's texts. But fans want *more*. They want to *be* the creator. And so they (well, we) have taken the text into their own hands.

To be a creator, fans must create new material that is analogous to the canon material. By creating fan canon (fanon), communities (or sometimes BNFs) rise to that equivalency; fanon can become so well accepted that some fans don't even know it's not from the original text, and sometimes creators even work it into later, actual canon material.[2] Pilgrimages offer fans the experience of physically becoming a creator by allowing fans to experience firsthand the true materials the creator used—Austen's writing desk, Colin Firth's white shirt—and therefore become closer to the canon material. On top of the physical closeness, fans can prove their level of fannish-ness by lording it over other fans that only *they* have been to the *true* location, or touched the *true* material, or been in contact with the *real* creator.[3] (The hidden references called "easter eggs" often serve much the same purpose, a process of testing other fans that is often called "gatekeeping.") And, of course, fans can take canon material and twist it. Although fanfiction is a large part of reimagining canon material, the internet has provided a more compact way: memes. By adapting a currently popular meme to fit a particu-lar fandom, fans remix canon material and create miniaturized adaptations,[4] allowing new fans to understand the canon via proxy.

Fanon can be a multilayered thing, spanning many fans across genera-tions, or it can be a simple concept that takes a fandom by storm and is never altered. Within media fandom there is a lot of fanon that revolves around the concept of an actor in some way becoming the character they portray. Tony Stark and Robert Downey Jr. being the "same person" is a common idea that has leaked from being a joke to becoming a part of fanfiction and Real Person Fic (RPF). Chris Evans, who portrays Captain America, has been called by his fictional superhero name in major media outlets,[5] as well as by fans. This crossing of the streams between personhood and fictional portrayal can deeply influence an actor's career, as fans hold tight to the idea that a certain actor *is* their fictional portrayal.[6] Within Austen canon something very similar has happened, but along with the fanon becoming the conflation of actor and character, a very specific scene was added in one adaptation and has become the epitome of fan canon within the fandom. We'll explore this moment and track this piece of fanon from its inception to the present day and its im-mersion into almost canon material, as well as where it leads us as we move through to gatekeeping and remixing.

Fans are smart people. They can figure out the twist in TV shows before they happen (such as purgatory in *Lost* or most of the twists in *Westworld*), they run fan-made wikis that creators turn to for reminders, and they create works that can be even more powerful than the original. But creators need to be ex-plicit about what the world is and how it operates for fans to be able to do any of this. With muddied distinctions fans are kept out of the sandbox, unsure of what counts and what doesn't count. They can't create fanon, let alone memes and other fan-made content.

Following the rip-roaring success of *The Lizzie Bennet Diaries*, the company Pemberley Digital announced that they would tackle perhaps the most difficult-to-adapt Austen novel, *Emma*. The adaptation placed Emma Woodhouse as a lifestyle coach, Harriet as her deeply anxious assistant, and Mr. Knightley (Alex instead of George in this adaptation) as her business partner. James Elton became someone running for state senate, and his eventual wife crossed over from *The Lizzie Bennet Diaries* and was Caroline Lee (*LBD*'s version of Caroline Bingley). Emma ran a fashion blog and answered Q&As about her lifestyle coaching, the characters had social media accounts, and it was presented as the same sort of transmedia experience as *LBD*, but it immediately felt different. The Austen adaptations surge in the 1990s and 2000s produced more than one *Emma* adaptation, high-waisted dresses and well-trimmed breeches and all, but *Clueless* was really the only adaptation to hit the nail on the head in terms of acknowledging the type of person Emma Woodhouse truly is: a busybody who truly believes that she is better than anyone else. Austen uses ironic language (we talk about this later in chapter 7) to indicate that the novel doesn't take Emma too seriously, but the self-seriousness of adaptations outside of *Clueless* can make for difficult watching without this important aspect. *Emma Approved* fell into this same trap, but taking Emma Woodhouse too seriously was just the start of the adaptations' problems: they didn't create any in- and out-world distinctions.

The Lizzie Bennet Diaries was completely in-world; all questions asked were things that the characters could see, all videos that existed on the channel were things that other characters could be watching, and they did. Q&A videos involved real fans playacting and asking questions as a part of the story, and the characters interacted with each other in real time on Twitter and Tumblr. *Emma Approved* appeared to be the same style of adaptation on the surface: Emma had cameras installed in everyone's office and collected footage all the time (apparently for a future video about how amazing she and her company are). Yet the characters didn't seem to know that the videos were being released, even if they knew that they were being filmed at their desks.

Rather than bringing the audience in or excluding them completely, *Emma Approved* chose a middle ground. The videos for the series, which were released on a schedule, were supposedly based on the footage collected by Emma but cut together and released by . . . well, it was never clear. The other characters, it turns out, couldn't see the videos, and they didn't exist "in-world," only "out-world," meaning that only the audience could see them. Yet the videos were posted on Emma's Twitter and Tumblr. Q&As became increasingly confusing as people submitted questions in the same style that they had in *Lizzie Bennet Diaries*, asking about the story, playing along, only to have their questions ignored because it turns out that the characters wouldn't have known that those things were in the public eye.

Fans can make a story out of anything, but they need structure. When a story is unclear, fans are going to fade away; with so many different types of media vying for attention, it can be easy to drop even a beloved story if things don't make sense anymore.

It quickly became clear that fans were having this exact problem. The producers attempted to clear up the issue by talking through a few of these fan questions in their FAQ page (as of January 2018 still not updated): "Q: Are Emma's Videos 'in world'? A: . . . But the short answer is no. Every video or reference to a video is out of world."[7] and expanded on the answer on a special page that was needed to make sure that the borders between our world and their world were made clear:

- Emma knows she is recording herself.

- Emma's friends and clients are aware that Emma is recording many things.

- They are not aware that their videos are being posted on the internet, because to them they are not for public consumption.

- Emma's public channel and Pemberley Digital's channel are out of world to her and the other characters.

- Basically, everything that's a video OR that is a piece of social media referencing a video is out of world. Everything else is in world.[8]

In some ways, this cleared things up for fans, but even Bernie Su, head writer and showrunner, had difficulty creating an understandable break-down. For instance, in Emma Woodhouse's world there are no public videos; these have been put together by—our world? But in the FAQ Bernie Su writes that "Emma's co-workers and friends (Knightley, Harriet, Annie, Ryan, etc.) do not know that there are public videos of them,"[9] but he has already explicitly stated that the videos, any video at all, is out-world, meaning that in the world of *Emma Approved* there aren't any videos anyway, so there wouldn't be any public videos.

This may seem like making mountains out of molehills—after all, at a certain point an audience member who has read the FAQ (although they would have to specifically seek it out rather than giving up on a confusing premise) can say, "I don't get why this works the way it does, but I can roll with it." But I, for one, never got to that point. Even though TV shows such as *The Office* and *Parks and Rec* had popularized the mockumentary (mock documentary) style of filming, this was clearly something different, as the characters didn't know that this was going to be released. Every time a character would acknowledge the camera I was pulled out of the fiction: Why would Emma Woodhouse's Twitter have a tweet about a new video if they weren't for public consumption? When were these videos being released? Who edited them? *Why didn't her employees sue her if she eventually released this footage?* Audiences and readers ignore plot holes and suspend disbelief for hundreds of problems in literature, but at a certain point the audience can no longer do so. The producers were clearly aware of this, providing longer answers than the one above (that is, the TL;DR[10] version), yet fans still had issues with following and buying the story. *LA Weekly* interviewed some fans and one fan put it perfectly, "Sure, there's the main site with the update of the week, but by going through it *I feel like it breaks the illusion of reality, which is really my favorite part*" (emphasis mine).[11] This break in the reality of the story removes so much of the ironic components.

When fans can't understand how a story fits together they don't create fan content. There is fan content for *Emma Approved* (93 works on Archive of Our Own, for instance), but compare that to the 1,067 listed under *Lizzie Bennet Diaries*.[12] These aren't quite equivalencies, as *Emma Approved* never reached the popularity heights that *The Lizzie Bennet Diaries* did, but that begs the question why, and did this in-/out-world confusion factor in? Fan canon (fanon) is built on the understanding of the worlds a story inhabits. The world has structure and meaning and logic (even if the logic is that it's crazy). Fanon has to make *sense* in a world, has to be buyable by the rest of the fan community to reach that echelon, and when there is confusion built into where the world lives in regards to the characters, or lapses in logic regarding what characters do and don't understand, it creates holes in the logic that fan canon doesn't fill. With *Emma Approved*'s issues the audience and fan base don't have the understanding and distinction that the larger Austen fandom does to create fanon.

So in a fandom as old as Austen's, how *does* fanon get created? Consider Mr. Darcy (as we all should). So much of Mr. Darcy's appeal to modern audiences revolves around his visual allure, yet according to historians, Mr. Fitzwilliam Darcy would have been thin with an oval face and a pointy jaw (no square jaw to be seen), slim sloping shoulders in contrast to his strong legs, and frustratingly to many fans, a small chest without the rippled torso of Colin Firth. And he would have worn a powdered wig—no invitingly dark curls to be blown in the wind or gather sweat while dancing.[13] Yet we do not see a thin, weak-chested man when we look at adaptations throughout the eras;[14] we see muscled men with dark hair and a square jaw. Where did this come from? There is no archived footage of the first filmed (in this case, televised) adaptation of *Pride and Prejudice* from 1938, but the actor, Andrew Osborn, was a brunet with a broad chest and wide shoulders.[15] Significantly, the BBC, who later created the most recognizable Mr. Darcy with his brown hair, square jaw, and triangular torso, produced this first adaptation, and whether or not they knew that Mr. Darcy's portrayal was incorrect doesn't matter.[16] Jane Austen never gave a description more than "Mr. Darcy soon drew the attention of the room by his fine, tall person, handsome features, noble mien, and the report which was in general circulation within five minutes after his entrance, of his having ten thousand a year."[17] Just as J. K. Rowling never described Hermione's skin color, allowing fans to embrace a darker-skinned Hermione than depicted in the films and cover art,[18] fans can take unsaid information and fill in the blanks as they please. The BBC did just that. Although it's perhaps a stretch to categorize an entire company as a "fan," given the number of adaptations of Austen works they have produced since 1938 (seventeen, including six of *Pride and Prejudice* alone[19]), we are going to categorize them as such.

The BBC's envisioning of Mr. Darcy so heavily influenced successive adaptations that the BBC's depiction became canon—there are no blond Darcys to be found.[20, 21] In 1995 the BBC added another piece to that depiction, and one that fans accepted so much that it became fanon and was then used in their own material;[22] Colin Firth was cast as Mr. Darcy. His depiction of Mr. Darcy has become so tied to the character that fans have incorporated him into countless imaginings and have even created a word to denote the type of relationship that Colin Firth portrayed. ("Firthing" is defined as "the act of hanging around the object of your affections looking intense but never actually telling them how you feel."[23]) Colin Firth has become so wrapped up in Mr. Darcy that basically no news article mentioning Firth skips a mention of his role in the adaptation; he has never escaped this early career success, and this is, in part, due to his fans.[24] His role just a few years later as Mark Darcy in *Bridget Jones's Diary* (an adaptation of the novel of the same name, which is in turn an adaptation of *Pride and Prejudice*) further cemented his role as the ur-Darcy.[25]

Okay. So Colin Firth played Mr. Darcy in one "true" adaptation and one derivative adaptation. So what?

Well, for one, Colin Firth, as he will remind you, is not Mr. Darcy.[26] He portrayed the official Mr. Darcy in just one adaptation. And yet fans, including authors of other adaptations, constantly use his image, his portrayal, and his name in conjunction with the character. *Lost in Austen*, for instance, includes the character Elizabeth Bennet using images of Colin Firth as images of her husband "and Amanda having a 'postmodern moment,' asking Mr. Darcy to re-enact Firth's Darcy's famous swim."[27] *The Lizzie Bennet Diaries* references Colin Firth's role as Mark Darcy in *Bridget Jones's Diaries* while talking about their version of Mr. Darcy. Even when characters are separated drastically by time and space, characters played by Colin Firth are connected to Mr. Darcy as Cartmell is with Firth's performance in *A Single Man* (2009).[28]

When the casting for the 2005 film version of *Pride and Prejudice* was announced, the Austen fans were . . . displeased.[29] Liz, from Manchester, wrote in "There is only one Mr. Darcy and that is Colin Firth. Thank God for DVD!" A Spanish fan commented, "I can't imagine other [sic] actor playing Mr Darcy but Colin Firth. He 'is' the one and only Mr Darcy." Some fans were more positive, but still defaulted to the idea that Colin Firth remains the standard: "Nobody can beat Colin Firth—he was made for the role and played it perfectly. I'm sure that Macfadyen will do a good job, but doubt it will be a patch on Colin Firth—had me swooning on the sofa!" Travis, who added "Pride and Prejudice devotee" to his location as a part of his comment, noted, "Colin Firth took the role of Fitzwilliam Darcy and made it his own, Matthew Macfadyen will have to go along [sic] way to match Firth let alone beat him. I do not envy his task, but I wish him all the best."

In the end, Matthew Macfadyen did an admirable job, although he admitted that he'd never read the novel nor seen the two most famous adaptations (Laurence Olivier and Colin Firth).[30] Yet he is not known for portraying "the" Mr. Darcy in the larger Austen fandom; even today it's Colin Firth who wears that mantle. A Google image search turns up a good mix of both Macfadyen and Firth, though it leans to Firth. It's interesting, too, that Jennifer Ehle never had the "always Lizzie Bennet" hanging over her head. Perhaps because she did not go on to be quite as well known? A few comments from the BBC forum in particular point out a possible reason why Firth can't seem to separate himself from Mr. Darcy: "Give me Colin Firth in a wet shirt getting out of a pond anyday. Swoon. . . . Nothing will ever beat that scene of Colin Firth with his shirt dripping wet. Pure lust on legs! . . . Macfadyen probably won't look so good in a wet shirt either."[31] Partway through the famous six-part 1995 miniseries is a moment that never existed in the canon text. Mr. Darcy (Colin Firth), coming home from London, exhausted, rides onto his estate and takes a moment to strip off his outer layers and take a dive into a pond. He swims for a bit and then emerges, dripping, his oversized wet shirt clinging to, as the *New York Times* put it, his "rippled torso." He begins walking back to his house, only to run into Elizabeth, who is wandering the grounds during her tour of the property. The moment, Darcy in a state of undress,[32] Elizabeth's overwhelming feelings as a result of the estate and her own internal struggles, has become a permanent fixture for fans.

In a text where every moment of eye contact, every incidental touch, every carefully placed word can mean so much more, the BBC, in their fannish wisdom, stripped Mr. Darcy down to his underwear and presented him to the love of his life. New fans coming to the novel from the adaptation are shocked[33] to find that that famous scene? It's not canon. And it's not just casual fans. Benedict Cumberbatch, another fan-favorite actor, "dressed as Mr. Darcy"[34] for a charity photoshoot in 2014—did he get on horseback or wear breeches and go hunting or pose before a big castle? Nope. He stripped down to an (oversized) white undershirt and hopped into a pond. A scene which never happened in canon but which is now so ingrained with *Pride and Prejudice* and Mr. Darcy that an unconnected celebrity donned a costume not to look like Mr. Darcy but to look like Colin Firth *playing* Mr. Darcy. The pond dive/Colin Firth as Mr. Darcy fanon doesn't end there, either. In 2013 a twelve-foot fiberglass statue of the cinematic moment was erected in Hyde Park, London,[35] and toured the UK before ending in Lyme Park, Cheshire, home of the original shooting location.[36] The shirt Colin Firth wore even ended up in an exhibit at the Folger Shakespeare Library for diehards to visit, although it has since left the museum.[37]

And the screenplay writer, Andrew Davies? The fan that truly started it all? He meant it as a headcanon;[38] he meant the scene to be a moment that he imagined Darcy would take, a situational moment based on both Darcy and Elizabeth's characters: "It was about Darcy being a bloke, diving in his lake on a hot day, not having to be polite—and then he suddenly finds himself in a situation where he does have to be polite. So you have two people having a stilted conversation and politely ignoring the fact that one of them is soaking wet. I never thought it was supposed to be a sexy scene in any way."[39] Exactly the same process that any other fan might go through to create a headcanon that gets picked up and turned around and becomes fanon. The final nail in the coffin for Colin Firth ever escaping his role as Mr. Darcy.

The BBC created Colin Firth's Mr. Darcy, and as perhaps the biggest fans around, we've categorized them as a BNF (Big Name Fan). But in some cases a lot of being a BNF and everything that goes with it—fanon, getting to go/going on pilgrimages, recognizing easter eggs, being the arbiter of what is "true"—is based on a fandom concept referred to as "gatekeeping." Within fandom, gatekeeping is a prescriptive definition of fandom[40] and is the process by which a fan or group of fans police who is allowed within a community. In some cases it takes the form of a test or demand of fan history, but it always revolves around a deep knowledge or closeness to a creator or creation. Fanon can get tied up in this process, as fans demand proof of knowledge and sometimes use the ability to spot the hidden references called "easter eggs" as a gatekeeping test.

(An important note is that although Austen scholars, and scholars in general, have a form of gatekeeping [do you have a masters degree? PhD? Where did you go to school?], we are specifically talking about the nonacademic fandom around Austen and the gatekeeping within that fandom. There is a deep tension between scholars and fans in all fandoms, which has its own gatekeeping tensions and could fill a book of its own.)

Gatekeeping revolves around a deep knowledge base and often is perceived as being close to the original object of fandom, but a lot of the role of BNFs *is* gatekeeping. BNFs are the fans that everyone looks to as the "authorities" on a particular fandom, and the BBC fits right into that. In this case the BBC does not continue to arbiter what truly is Austen and what isn't, at least as a corporation, but what it *does* do is provide a BNF-approved template—the 1995 *Pride and Prejudice* miniseries—for what Austen adaptations *should* be. Fans routinely judge other adaptations on the first "true" version, as seen in the comments mentioned earlier. But with Austen being so long deceased, and not having any direct descendants, who else could be authorities *but* the fans, including the BBC?[41]

With Austen gatekeeping happens, but in a slightly different way than it did with Twilight, for example. In Austen fandom, some of the fan spaces such as The Republic of Pemberley[42] and the Derbyshire Writers' Guild[43] are literally moderated. The moderators aren't necessarily scholars or experts but are seen as such because they either have been doing this for a long time, have been appointed by another BNF, or have passed a gatekeeping test. To be a part of these communities you have to post fanfiction within certain guidelines. Sure, anyone could post Austen fan material and creations online (and they do), but it may not go anywhere or be widely recognized within the fandom until it gets picked up by a BNF. If we, the authors of this book, post an Austen fic on Tumblr, it could be found by someone searching tags or following us. But it's more likely to spread if it gets reblogged by one of the "big" Austen blogs, such as KC in PA (we'll talk about them in a bit).

Another issue of gatekeeping is the location of fanon or fanart or fic; is it more likely to get attention if someone posts on fanfiction.net or AO3 (Archiveofourown.org) or if they go to an Austen-specific site? Holly rarely goes to the general fanfic sites *if* a fandom-specific site exists, as they are generally better moderated and because she feels like she's getting better quality because it's being "vetted" by someone. Zoe tends to stick with AO3, but mostly out of habit and laziness, and has had success in fandom-specific sites when looking for fic to read or research. Gatekeeping might look different in such an old fandom as compared to *Twilight* or even to comics, but it's still there and it's still a larger fandom issue.[44]

Fanon, headcanons, and fic, BNF approved or not, are all creation, and in the case of the 1995 BBC production, creation on a massive, canon-building scale. People flock not only to the statue of Colin Firth/Mr. Darcy or to the formerly wet shirt but also to the locations of filming to be a part of the production. The larger fanon context is always about creation. In many cases, because a headcanon usually passes through so many fans before it becomes fanon, it is often a piece that could potentially be something from canon; it's a reasonable moment or scene or character that *could* appear in the world created by the *original* author. It's *in character*. But not all fan creation—in fact, very little fan creation—goes through this wider process. Most fans are producing content for themselves and a few others.

Every time a fan writes a piece of fanfiction or draws fanart or exposits a theory to another fan, the next person down the line has the option to accept the extra material and add to it even more. This daisy chain of information can extend for so long that sometimes the final product looks nothing like the original (as happened in the chain of *Pride and Prejudice* to *Bridget Jones's Diary* to the movie of the same name to the sequel *Bridget Jones's Baby*), but sometimes it hits a nerve, and whether or not it becomes fanon, it resonates with fans. Memes[45] fall into this category.

The concept of memes has been around for a long time,[46] but with the internet the explosion of types of memes has gone critical. Places like Imgur, Tumblr, and Reddit are breeding grounds for memes. Something as simple as two people having a conversation referencing Edgar Allan Poe's "The Cask of Amontillado" can become a widespread-enough meme that major news outlets find the need to comment.[47]

Because of the widespread nature of memes, they can be highly adaptable. A popular meme that cycled through the internet in 2015 imagined a date and ran as follows:

> Person A: a basic question
>
> Person B: an answer that does not match Person A's opinion on the topic
>
> Person A: *shoving breadsticks into my purse* I'm sorry I have to leave[48]

This meme was highly personalizable, and fans went nuts. It became a shorthand way for fans to express a specific opinion (that a character or situation was good or bad, that they believed a certain thing, etc.) and it was so customizable that any fandom could, and did, latch on. Although the meme is quite old now, it has been incorporated into other memes and people are still using it as shorthand in all its eventual forms, which included many variants.[49]

For instance, a Jane Austen version of this meme runs as follows:

> **me, on a date**: so, have you read Pride and Prejudice?
>
> **them**: no, who reads classical literature anyway
>
> **me, shoving breadsticks into my purse**: i'm sorry but you have proven that you are the last person i could be prevailed upon to date[50] (emphasis in original)

Memes, even highly specific ones, can be altered to fit a fandom or person quite easily on the whole,[51] and so one could learn about a fandom by examining it through these lenses. By looking at, for instance, the breadsticks meme, one could examine the most popular posts on Tumblr and Reddit that have this format and be able to chart where fans and—if there are enough posts—entire fandoms sit on a specific fan or general issue. Memes, essentially remixed canon, provide a shorthand for new fans to see what a story is about. Many memes, text- or image-based, and recently (although the app has since ceased to exist) via Vine, have been adapted in this way, but there is one meme that did this for Austen in a more successful way than others: the On-ion headline meme.

On the face of it the Onion headline meme is quite simple. It's a headline from the satirical publication the Onion laid over a screenshot or image from, generally, a movie or TV show. The meme probably began as an offshoot of an earlier meme referred to as the "cinnamon roll meme," in which the phrase "Beautiful Cinnamon Roll Too Good For This World, Too Pure,"[52] also original-ly an Onion headline, and variants were used to describe characters.[53] From there, some users used Onion headlines in combination with stock photos (which are, themselves, a meme), and two users on Tumblr (kcinpa and what-wouldelizabethbennetdo) thought of using Onion headlines splashed across screenshots from various Austen adaptations. Because the Onion's headlines are often either highly specific or highly general and have a known and un-derstood social connotation, combining them with a screenshot from Aus-ten allows fans who understand Austen to get the inside joke but also allows non-Austen fans to apply the lens "Onion headlines" and extrapolate what the Austen screenshot is talking about. The images are, essentially, miniature modernizations.

As an example, one screenshot from the 1995 BBC adaptation of *Pride and Prejudice* shows Elizabeth holding the letter from Mr. Darcy and looking down at it. The Onion headline superimposed over the side of the image reads: "I've Left My Haltingly Awkward Voice Message; Now The Ball's In Her Court."[54] (See figure 1 for a perfect modernization of that moment.)

Within today's social context, this photo makes sense. The reader can infer that the letter is from a potential romantic partner, as the phrase "now the ball's in her court" is often used in dating, and Elizabeth looks quite non-plussed. For Austen fans and aficionados, the text adds a layer of humor to the situation. Darcy's letter is in many ways similar to a modern sitcom situation, and the awkwardness of the voicemail-and-run approach provides a moment of humor while also making the moment relatable. Many people have been the leaver or receiver of voicemails like the one implied by the Onion headline in question, and the social context adds an understanding of the character even an Austen scholar might not have understood previously. Another im-age (see figure 2), this time from the 2005 *Pride and Prejudice* adaptation, shows

Figure 1 "I've Left My Haltingly Awkward Voice
Message; Now The Ball's In Her Court." Meme courtesy
of whatwouldelizabethbennetdo (Tumblr).

Elizabeth Bennet looking extremely apprehensive and the hand of Mr. Collins
holding out a flower. The text? "Oh, God, Area Man Making His Move."[55]

The text perfectly encapsulates the clear thought in Elizabeth's facial ex-
pression and shows a modern audience that she's nervous in a very specific way. Many women who date men would recognize this headline as a valid
emotion, and would hope that Elizabeth had a way out of the conversation.
Again, too, the social context of Elizabeth's desperation to *not have this conversation* is powerfully replayed in the Onion headline text. "Area Man" is a
character that the Onion uses fairly often, and within our modern society the
phrase carries the connotation of an incredibly annoying, often overwhelm-
ingly frustrating, man; there is no better fit in Austen for "Area Man" than Mr.
Collins. With a text as old as *Pride and Prejudice*, much of the societal and social
context is lost on the nonhistorian. The photo mashup in figure 3 reinserts
this extra information while also providing a modern lens and, well, a laugh.

That laughter is important. Although students today may struggle with
the contextual humor in Austen, she's a riot. Take *Northanger Abbey*, a book that
most students read and think of as just about a swoon-happy woman who lets

Figure 2 "Oh, God, Area Man Making His Move."
Meme courtesy of K. C. Kahler (Tumblr: kcinpa).

Figure 3 "I'm Refreshingly Naïve!" Meme
courtesy of K. C. Kahler (Tumblr: kcinpa).

her imagination run away. But it's not! *Northanger Abbey* is based on, and satirizes, an entire genre: gothic literature.[56] Although Catherine is presented as a silly girl, Austen digs into each and every iconic trope of the genre, ranging from extreme emotions to fainting heroines to perceived supernatural events behind locked doors. The book seems simple and boring because it was *meant* to. Austen was joining Coleridge and Wordsworth in deriding the gothic, but where the men wrote editorials, Austen wrote a parody that also satirized contemporary attitudes toward women and reading.[57] (In many ways it's one of the funniest books I have ever read.) So much of this context is missing in classrooms and on film, where studios have made them often just feel like sweeping, period romances. But they're not.

It may sound silly, but these memes can help reinvigorate the understanding of Austen's humor. The recent adaptation *Love and Friendship*, which is of Austen's epistolary novella *Lady Susan*, and not her juvenilia collection called "Love and Friendship," emphasizes the humor and biting wit found on the page,[58] rather than making a more staid version, but it's a rarity in the pantheon of adaptations. For *Northanger Abbey*, what the audience needs is a blatant understanding of what Austen was trying to say when she first wrote the novel. Good news: Kcinpa has us covered with a *Northanger Abbey*–Onion mashup.[59]

Those who have never read Austen or seen an adaptation can understand what these memes mean; the fans who created this have not only remixed the canon material but they have created an adaptation and even a teaching tool. By pairing contextualized Onion headlines with these screenshots they have put together a shortcut for the story. Possibly more important, the meme has brought back some of the humor inherent in Jane Austen but that modern audiences might not understand. Students or fans or even literary scholars can study these memes as a lens into how modern society views Austen, but they can also recontextualize Austen as a lens on today's society. We haven't changed all that much—we recognize the emotions and situations from over two hundred years ago and we can *relate* to them!

Unfortunately, these memes are still a part of the gatekeeping phenomenon that plagues fandom. Although they're amazing, and anyone could make them in a way, it is a format that *is* moderated. Anyone could make them, sure, but there are "official" accounts for them, specifically kcinpa. This was on a recognized news/pop culture site and has a list of news outlets that reported their success listed on their master post (where all their Onion-Austen mashups are linked).[60]

Fanon is not much different than memes in this way. Fanon allows modern fans, or fans throughout the years, to connect to the original canon text by expanding it and connecting with one another. The video "Dear Mr Darcy,"[61] for instance, depicts two women in approximate period dress rapping about how they would like Mr. Darcy to spend more time in a wet white shirt, but it also makes a joke about how the moment that the entire song is based on—the entire premise of the video—isn't canon. And yet the women, who are obviously modern and not trying to be period accurate, talk through every point about Mr. Darcy's personality not trumping his desirability that every woman seems to make through the years.[62] The video highlights the fact that fans, especially in Austen's fandom, really have to create their own additional content. After all, Jane isn't going to write it for them. To keep participating, to keep the fandom fresh, to give other fans more, more, more to interact with? That's going to have to come from fans, whether they're amateurs on Tumblr or pros at movie studios. Because of this, fan creations can also (and have) become part of the accepted canon. But that acceptance in Austen canon has a price: you have to make it big on your own, or you have to be willing to go through an arbiter, a gatekeeper, or a BNF.

In many ways memes *should* be able to get around the gatekeeping issue while still also allowing fans to create more and more content, as memes can be so easily manipulated and adjusted to fit a specific fandom. And yet the meme that hit it big was the Onion/Austen headline meme, and although it was just started by "just a fan," kcinpa has been featured on a number of websites and has openly admitted that they aren't the only one who created this: Tumblr user whatwouldelizabethbennetdo created them at the same time but has received none of the fame. Instead the meme went through a bigger fan, a bigger outlet—and reached more people. There's always a silver lining.

Since Jane Austen isn't going to be writing us any new stories unless there's some sort of zombie experiment gone wrong, it's up to the fan community—from the BBC down to the new fan who has only watched the 2005 *Pride and Prejudice* adaptation—to help fill in the gaps. The gaps range from queer representation to fleshing out background characters to the best way to modernize *Mansfield Park*. In some cases that will happen in closed, gatekept communities such as *The Republic of Pemberley* or at conferences like the Jane Austen Society of North America. In other cases fans are already hard at work on Tumblr,[63] Twitter,[64] and Archive of Our Own,[65] perhaps not creating the next 1995 BBC *Pride and Prejudice* adaptation but creating fanon and fanart and fanfiction and expanding the world of Jane Austen as they see fit.

2

As If!
Clueless and the Modern AU

HOLLY   Okay, so you're probably going, is this, like, a Noxzema commercial or what?
But I actually have a way normal life for a teenage girl.
—Cher Horowitz, *Clueless*

We cannot talk about Austen adaptations without mentioning
one of the most groundbreaking films of the Austen megaverse:
Clueless.[1] Released during the height of Austenmania in the 1990s,
Clueless was the first of its kind in many ways. A stunning example
of the modern AU— or alternate universe—fanfiction, the film
completely transforms the setting of *Emma*, placing the story in
the dramatic, plaid- and platform-filled world of the Beverly Hills
teenager. It was a formula that countless other Austen films have
tried to recapture, from the Bollywood *Bride and Prejudice* to the
religious *Pride and Prejudice: A Latter Day Comedy*. What *Clueless* does so
well, that arguably other Austen adaptations fail to accomplish at
the same level, is maintain the ironic satire so particular to Austen's narration (*Emma* in particular emphasizes the irony). Most
films, because of the removal of her wry narrator, fail to fully
translate Austen's mockery of the romantic and societal conventions within which her characters are forced to operate. *Clueless*,
with Cher Horowitz standing in as scene narrator and director
Amy Heckerling's keen desire to translate not just the *story* but the
spirit of *Emma*, manages to be funny, ironic, and romantic, all at
the same time. Heckerling's film must operate within the expected conventions of a teenage-focused romantic comedy, but using
Austen's novel as a base, it is able to poke fun at the genre, and
lay groundwork for similar, female-led comedy films to follow. In
fact, the film is so well translated that it stands on its own. It did
not even need to bill itself as an Austen adaptation: it was remarkably successful just as a teen rom-com. So successful, in fact, that

over twenty years later, people are still watching it, talking about it, and memeing it.

Clueless is a film that has become a touchstone for a generation—those who were teenagers at the time of its release (and in the years following, like we were), and for Austen fans. Hitting the big screen during the height of the 1990s Austenmania, a decade that saw the release of seven major Austen-related films or miniseries—including two additional, more traditional *Emma* films—*Clueless* tapped into a convergence of several different pop culture trends at once: Austen films, teen films, and third-wave feminism. Directed and written by a woman, starring women, and focused almost entirely on women's stories, the film was a near-perfect update of Austen's novel. Cher Horowitz, a popular, attractive teenager so convinced of her own rightness and ability to read others, meddles in the lives of her friends and teachers, believing herself to be at once totally tapped into what everyone else wants, but also above the drama herself. In the end, she learns that not only was she wrong about most of the people around her but, most important, she was wrong about herself. Mixed into this journey of self-discovery is a witty, sharp homage to the culture of excess of the 1990s, a thoughtful portrayal of female empowerment and friendships, and the ironic Austen narrator embodied by Cher herself (through voiceover) and occasionally through the viewers (that is, through the camera lens).

In keeping with Austen's tradition, *Clueless*'s narrative focuses entirely on the women's stories. The story is essentially Cher's, and her close relationships are also almost all women. Her best friend Dionne, her protege Tai, and her teacher Mrs. Geist all share significant screen time with Cher, and they heavily influence her life and decisions. While men are, of course, present, their lives are second to the women's, and their positions in Cher's life are defined by their relationship to her or other women around her. The men in the film function more as objects to help tell the women's stories than as fully developed characters themselves. Her father, Mel, fills the role of demanding, protective father who cares deeply about his daughter, even if he is a little rough around the edges. Josh, her ex-stepbrother and love interest (it's a little icky), is a smart, image-eschewing college guy. Murray and Travis serve as love interests for Dionne and Tai, respectively. Mr. Hall, Cher's debate teacher, is little more than comedic relief and a love interest for Mrs. Geist.

The women, on the other hand, play major roles in Cher's life. Dionne is her best friend, supporting her decisions and being the one other person who Cher most relates to in her life. They dress similarly (a clear sign from the costume design team that these two should be seen as equals), have similar life experiences, and are always, always there for each other. Tai begins as her project, but transforms into her friend once Cher learns to stop meddling in her life. Like Harriet in *Emma*, Cher takes on Tai as someone whose life she can improve with her superior influence, acting almost like a teacher. As the narrative progresses, however, Cher learns to appreciate all of her friends, Tai included, for their unique, special attributes. By the end, Cher and Tai have become equals rather than mentor/mentee, as evidenced partly by their sharing a table at Mrs. Geist's wedding to Mr. Hall—and by the similarities in their attire, such as wearing complementary colors. Mrs. Geist, who like Mr. Hall is one of Cher's teachers, also has a profound influence on her. Unlike Mr. Hall, who is present but does not impact Cher's journey of self-discovery, Mrs. Geist is the teacher Cher chooses to emulate when she decides to "make over her soul." Volunteering to help with a philanthropy project headed by Mrs. Geist, Cher has obviously chosen her as a model for herself as a woman she would like to become more like. This can also be seen in contrast to her earlier attempts to emulate her father by using her "powers of persuasion" to argue her way to better grades. At the beginning of the film, she follows her father's framework to argue for the *appearance* of improvement. At the end, she looks to Mrs. Geist as a model of how to actually become a better person. Women, much more than men, are at the heart of *Clueless*, the same way that Austen, in her time, was concerned with telling the stories of women.

Clueless not only retains the spirit of Austen through its lens of telling women's stories, but is also manages to maintain her ironic narrator as well, something most Austen film adaptations fail to grasp. This is partially done through the use of Cher as an actual narrator. In scenes through the film, Cher will, in voiceover, offer commentary, context, or insight into what is happening on screen or in her head. One perfect example of this narration at once celebrating and skewering the social conventions the film portrays is in the very first few scenes. Set to the pop-punk sounds of "Kids in America" by the Muffs, the film opens with brightly colored titles, showing Cher and her friends driving, shopping, partying, and laughing. About a minute into the montage you hear Cher's voice: "Okay, so you're probably going, 'Is this like a Noxzema commercial or what?' But seriously, I actually have a way normal life for a teenage girl." This line, delivered perfectly straight by Alicia Silverstone, immediately does what Austen's narrator does: it lays out a supposed fact while at once undermining the authenticity of the statement. Cher goes on to point out that she gets up, brushes her teeth, and picks out her clothes for the day. On the surface this *sounds* like a typical high schooler's morning. When that is played over the image of Cher using a one-of-a-kind computer database to sort through her closet for the perfect outfit (and a database that will inform her if her selections are *gasp* mismatched), the resulting effect is both endearing and comical. Here is this adorable, clueless girl who thinks that the life she leads is ordinary, and we are about to see how absolutely un-ordinary it really is. But the film casts this critical eye on Cher's life while acknowledging that she is unlikable yet making her endearing without making her character unlikable, much like how modern audiences respond to canon Emma. Opening the film this way clues the audience in to what is to come: the film is going to be fun, and funny, while also paying sharp homage to the culture that Cher inhabits. The characters are not villainized for their lifestyles and choices but rather celebrated, with some skepticism and a bit of sarcasm.

And like Austen's novels, *Clueless* has continued to influence pop culture long after its initial release. It was a boundary-pushing film, both in its content and structure. In its depiction of an incredibly diverse cast, *Clueless* was one of the first forms of any media to feature characters of color and diverse sexualities as key parts of the cast. Dionne is a black woman and her boyfriend Murray, a black man. As mentioned previously, Dionne is created and portrayed as Cher's equal, in social status, attractiveness, and wealth. Her story is also not defined by her race. Her place in the story isn't to be a stereotypical, "token" black character. She is simply a character who happens to be black.

The film treats sexuality in a similar way, with one of the first appearances of a gay character in a feature film. We meet Christian, who Cher initially thinks of as a potential partner, but more because she feels she *should* be attracted to him rather than because she feels any romantic attraction. When Christian's sexuality is revealed (it is not explicitly stated at first), it is not treated as a dramatic moment, other than for Cher to realize that she misunderstood and misread his attention to her as something more than friendship. Cher is embarrassed because *she failed to correctly read the signs,* not because Christian is gay. In fact, once that has been revealed, it simply becomes part of Christian's character but not part of his story. Additionally, his character is allowed to be complex. He loves shopping and he dresses well, but he also stands up to Tai's bullies at the mall and is not presented as overly feminine in his mannerisms. He is given the complexity to be whoever he is, without judgment or recrimination from the characters. None of his friends treat him differently when they learn he is gay; they simply treat him like any other person of their acquaintance.

In addition to its willingness to confront race and sexuality as simply part of a contemporary culture, *Clueless* also helped push forward the ideals of third-wave feminism in the popular realm. A movement in the 1990s, third-wave feminism pushed the ideas that women could be at once feminine and feminist—that they did not have shun traditionally feminine things like high heels and makeup in order to identify with the empowerment of women. Women could "have a push-up bra and a brain at the same time."[2] *Clueless* truly embraced the notion for its female characters. Cher and Dionne are popular, attractive, and care about their clothing and appearance. Cher spends hours getting ready for a date and worries when Christian rejects her sexual advances that it was because her hair went flat or the lighting was bad. But these women also believe themselves to be equal to—maybe even superior to—the men in her life. She does not allow Josh or her father to dictate her clothing or activities. She never questions her place at the top of the high school food chain. She rejects the idea that just because Elton likes her, she somehow owes him her attention. Her inspiration, Emma, constantly meddles in what was traditionally the "masculine" sphere, and Cher follows in those footsteps.

Other supporting characters are given the same treatment as well. Mrs. Geist, for example, begins the film as the stereotypical frumpy teacher who cares less about her appearance or romantic prospects than she does about saving the world, or, at least, getting spoiled teenagers to care about people outside their bubble. But she is not treated as any *less* worthy of romance or respect because of her choices. Sure, Cher tries to give her a subtle "make-over" by adjusting the way she dresses and presents herself, but Mrs. Geist does not let herself be too impacted by this influence. Cher can take Mrs. Geist's glasses off and tie her cardigan around her shoulders, but Mrs. Geist continues to return to her frumpy appearance and zest for world-saving. By the end of the film, Cher is seeking to emulate more of Mrs. Geist's compassion for others but she also maintains her love of clothes and shopping. In *Clueless*, women are allowed to be complex creatures, not just one side of the spectrum or the other. In this respect, *Clueless* is a sharp reflection of the time period in which the film was being made, but it also translates Austen so well that it shows how timeless a novel like *Emma* is. She fits as well into 1995 as she does in 1815.

Like Austen's novels, *Clueless* was pushing the boundaries of what was being done during the time it was made. And also like Austen's novels, it continues to be referenced in pop culture today. Even though the film recently celebrated its twentieth anniversary, new fans continue to discover it, and old fans continue to salute the classic. Iggy Azalea, the Australian rapper, paid homage to the film in the music video for her breakout hit, "Fancy," from the costumes to the title credits to the re-creation of some of the most iconic scenes (like the gym class and driving-on-the-freeway scenes). Azalea said in interviews that she wanted to visually represent the "West Coast" sound of the song by pointing back to the quintessential West Coast culture portrayed in a film she loved growing up.[3] *Clueless*'s influence can also be seen in other media as well, including a "Modern Clueless" Twitter account, which offers a "Cher Horowitz" take on current events.[4] One of the most recurring references to the film, and it crops up on this Twitter account as well as across Tumblr, Pinterest, and other social media platforms, is Cher's famous speech in debate about whether the United States should be welcoming to refugees from other countries—still a hot debate twenty-three years later. Cher ends her speech by stating, "And in conclusion, may I please remind you that it does not say RSVP on the Statue of Liberty." Following heated exchanges around immigration and protection for undocumented immigrants in the US in recent years, thousands of tweets and posts have used a gif of this scene as a comedic, yet serious, reminder of their perspective of making the country more welcoming to those from other nations. The other gif/image that seemed to pop up frequently when I was browsing through *Clueless* memes on various sites was the film's famous catch phrase "As if!" to demonstrate a rejection of something. The dialogue of *Clueless* has simply permeated certain areas of pop culture to the point where it is just part of the vernacular now.[5]

Like many of Austen's works, *Emma* and *Clueless* have transcended their original context to become something more, something that people who would not necessarily describe themselves as Austen fans can understand or reference. In *Clueless* Amy Heckerling and the cast and crew seamlessly blended Austen's comedy of manners with a female-led teen comedy. So seamless, in fact, that many who have seen *Clueless* do not even find out until much later that it was based on a novel written 190 years before, by a single woman trying to break barriers around whose stories get told, and how women can support themselves in a world that told them they needed a man to do it for them. While Emma Woodhouse and Cher Horowitz occupied very different times and places, their lives are remarkably similar, and Austen's timeless narrative, characters, and themes were played out in a funny, entertaining, genre-breaking way almost two hundred years later, to audiences of women and girls who could see themselves in these strong, intelligent, complex women and feel empowered to pursue their own identities, no matter what they may be.

3

Obstinate, Headstrong Girls: Fanfiction as Feminist Practice

HOLLY

But for my own part, if a book is well written, I always find it too short.
—Jane Austen, *Northanger Abbey*

Jane Austen fanfic (JAFF), like in most fandoms, exists at the intersection of several different catalysts. First there are the lurkers who are just there to consume, perhaps occasionally share or comment, but prefer to experience fandom alone. Then you have the producers who want to rewrite or reimagine or extend the stories they love so much. Next are the fans who want the community: they love Austen and they want to find and interact with others who feel the same way they do. And within all of this you have a largely female audience, whose desires and experiences are historically underrepresented by the entertainment industry, regardless of media.

Austen's texts especially are primed for the resistance that fandom is known for because they were resistant themselves. Aja Romano notes that "fandom is subversive. If a canonical worldview is entirely straight-white-male, then fans will actively resist it."[1] Austen's novels are telling women's stories within the straight-white-male society in which she lived, so Austen fandom is an ideal space to continue to explore women, nonbinary people, and others who have felt that their experiences and voices are ignored by mainstream media. JAFF allows fans to tell the stories *they* want to tell, in the *ways* they want to tell them. As Henry Jenkins discusses, this practice of expanding on characters, stories, and events is more common among female fans than male fans.[2] One thing that makes the JAFF community unique, however, is that the canonical texts that fans are drawing from were written by a woman, suggesting that they are not inherently ignoring the female voice, as often happens with other media. Therefore, unlike in some fanfiction circles, women are not necessarily attempting to "reclaim feminine interests" through masculine texts.[3] Austen's texts *already* deal with feminine interests, though in a time different from our present day.

Fanfiction is often viewed as a deviant practice, and fan spaces are often female-centric, as they grew as a space for women creators and consumers who felt their voices and stories were ignored by mainstream media. Because Austen fanfiction sits at the intersection of these two spaces (women's stories and women's fan practices), writing and reading JAFF is an inherently feminist practice. Women take one woman's stories and create their own, often inserting modern values and ideals of womanhood and society into the texts and, occasionally, follow their fan writing along nontraditional paths to publishing that are more accessible to women and nonbinary writers. While some may argue against viewing Austen as a feminist writer herself, there is no doubt that fan spaces, especially fanfiction spaces, around Austen's canon today are doing feminist work.

JAFF also echoes a practice common during Austen's time, too. The process of writing letters in the nineteenth century, as Jenkins points out, was a way for women to maintain ties with other women, build community, and share concerns and experiences. Fanfiction writing, with its origins in postal mail, zines, and enclosed circles of friends, follows in the letter writing tradition.[4] Additionally, novels during Austen's time were often treated like the deviant culture that fanfiction plays in our contemporary world. Austen herself parodies the culture surrounding the gothic novel in *Northanger Abbey*, and one doesn't have to look far in any of her novels to see men disparaging novels or the women who read them. Novels were things that *women* read and *women* wrote because they were not as important as the historical, philosophical, religious, or even poetic, texts being produced largely by men. Austen's works provide a "bedrock on which other authors and fans develop their creativity and invention," especially women, who form the largest portion of her fan base.[5] JAFF, then, can be seen as assuming the role for many Austen fans today that novels filled for women at the time: it is something written by them, for them, and resistant to the expectations of what society says they *should* be. This only adds to the feminist nature of those writing and reading Austen fanfiction; they are using modern methods to continue in Austen's literary tradition.

My first real encounter with an Austen spin-off was Linda Berdoll's published series *The Darcys*. I cannot even recall how I first encountered it, but it sparked an obsession. I quickly read the *Fitzwilliam Darcy, Gentleman* trilogy by Pamela Aidan, which tells the events of *Pride and Prejudice* from the perspective of Mr. Darcy (and which I discuss more later). Then I found *The Jane Austen Book Club* and *Austenland*. The number of Austen-adjacent books I have read is (not so shamefully) high and does not even begin to put a dent in the mountains of free fanfiction and published works available for consumption. And, of course, that does not include the films that are adaptations of the texts, or original works themselves. Austen-related media comprises an extremely tangled web of free fanfiction, published novels, open web series produced by fans or independent media companies, and Hollywood-produced films and television series. Once you decide to explore outside of the strict, Austen-authored canon, the line becomes: Where do you stop? The sheer reality of *how much* media exists is exhausting to consider. The struggle to determine just how far down you want to dive is difficult, and you may find yourself wondering, *How could there be so many ways to tell the same stories? And why would people want to?* (A valid question, given Jane Austen's incomparable writing.)

Fanfic writers and readers are attracted to the genre for any number of reasons. Sometimes it's because they want to experience the story from another point of view, explore a relationship that they feel is not given enough time in the novel, imagine what a character's life might look like in modern-day society. Writers may also use fanfiction as a way of exploring their own identities and developing their own writing style, in a place free from pressure and constraints of the "real world" outside of fan communities.[6] Writers and readers of JAFF may seek out fanfic communities to write for themselves, for others, and just out of pure love for Austen's works and a desire to keep the story going.[7] Most commonly, readers and writers of JAFF echo a similar sentiment when asked why they seek out fanfiction, published works, art, films, etc.: they want more.

Jane Austen was groundbreaking during her time; she pursued writing as a profession at a time when women did not even have professions. Scholars have argued over Austen's status as a feminist writer (is she or isn't she?),[8] but it is hard to deny her place as one of the first women novelists to achieve the amount of recognition and appeal that she has claimed since her death. While Austen may not be around to write anymore (unless she is, indeed, a vampire,[9] writing under a pseudonym), her legacy continues through the fans. This long-standing fandom, with its prolific producers and creators, in addition to creating a uniquely feminist space has also challenged the arguably strict line between "fanfiction" and "for-profit" work. While fanfiction has traditionally operated as a gift economy,[10] as something that fans do out of love for a show, a book, a film, JAFF has complicated that history because several well-known, published Austen-related novels began as open fanfiction on sites like the Derbyshire Writers Guild. It was through interaction with the fandom—through readers clamoring for more chapters and encouraging the authors to publish their work—that these once strictly fanfiction pieces began crossing boundaries into published, and therefore, profitable, novels. There are other novels, too, that do not have a documented history as fanfiction but whose authors confess to being rabid Austen fans, like Shannon Hale, author of Austenland, who claims to be a "loyal reader" and counts herself as one of Austen's "best friends."[11] Still further complicating this are when production companies, like the BBC or Pemberley Digital, produce films or series as adaptations but could also be viewed, as discussed previously, as Big Name Fans themselves.[12] Certainly, not every single published work that falls under the Austen oeuvre should be called "fanfiction," but these additional factors break down the strict "money isn't involved or it isn't fanfiction" dichotomy that can be seen, and argued over, in many fan spaces. As Austen herself broke boundaries of women supporting themselves as writers, Austen fanfiction writers are breaking the barriers between fanfiction and profit in our modern society, a practice that is cropping up in other fandoms as well. Following in Austen's literary footsteps, using a "new" and "deviant" form of writing to address issues and stories that matter to them, JAFF writers and readers are pushing the boundaries of fan writing practices and writing their own, women-centric, rules.

The Tangled Web of JAFF

Fanfiction has a much longer history than the modern internet, or even Jane Austen. While the proliferation of online communities (and changing attitudes about fan-created works) has certainly allowed fanfiction to flourish in ways never achieved before, writers have been borrowing characters and worlds and reworking them for centuries. In the most basic sense, fanfiction is defined as writing produced by fans of a particular media, based on plotlines, characters, or even settings within the story. Many fans also require that it not be produced for profit, but as we will explore in this chapter, that is a distinction that is less and less clear as fan practices and publishing converge. Fan writing, as a practice of taking someone else's work and rewriting or extending it, has a long, messy history. One clever Tumblr user, tjmystic, pointed out that works such as *Paradise Lost* and *The Divine Comedy* are essentially fanfictions of the book of Genesis and Catholic doctrine, respectively.[13] Constance Grady explains that, historically, borrowing characters and stories and rewriting was "just how storytelling worked."[14] She goes on to describe five famous works of literature that could be termed "fanfiction": *The Aeneid* (Virgil), *The Divine Comedy* (Dante), *Le Morte D'Arthur* (Mallory), *Hamlet* (Shakespeare), and *Wide Sargasso Sea* (Rhys). All of these famous works draw from at least one—some of them up to three—previously existing stories, and are examples of more traditional affirmational fanfiction. In the case of *The Aeneid*, it is the story of a minor character from Homer's *The Iliad*, whose life and story are continued after the end of the canon work. (In this way, it could be termed "affirmational fanfiction," as it extends part of the story but remains within the established canon world.[15])

Fanfiction clearly has a long history, though certainly no one at the time of the writing called *The Aeneid* fanfic. It is only through looking back on the history of what fan writers often call "playing in someone else's sandbox" that we can begin to see how much of the history of storytelling is, in a sense, a history of fanfiction. It is also important to note that fanfiction as a practice has a particularly gendered history, with women being the primary producers. This has led some to argue that the undervaluing of fan labor has much to do with this history. As Anne Jamison argues in *Fic*, women write fanfiction, but when men write "fic-like stories in fic-like ways," they call it "pastiche" and get published in the *Times*.[16]

Prior to the rise of the digital fan, much of modern fanfiction sharing was limited to conventions, zines, or a close group of friends.[17] The first large on-line fan community that created fanfiction as we see it today was probably the *Harry Potter* fandom; the series coincided with the rise of the internet and was a series read widely by both adults and young adults.[18] But now fan communities exist on the internet for almost any media entity, from Marvel Comics and *Harry Potter* to Austen and *Legend of Zelda*. These communities use websites such as fanfiction.net, Tumblr, Reddit, Wattpad, and more to write anything from novel-length stories, to headcanons, to drabbles,[19] to fics.[20]

Each type of fanfiction usually falls into one of two major categories: affirmational (following canon rules) or transformational (alternative universe, out of character, non-canon).[21] Transformational fanfiction is usually written to fix or right a wrong in the story in the eyes of the fans; in many cases this type of fiction adds romance where there wasn't romance previously[22] or removes—or adds—a character death. In addition to changing characters or stories or correcting what fans see as a gap or problem with the plot, fanfiction communities also provide opportunities for writers to speak with often unheard voices, using fanfic as a way to insert their own voices and experiences into a narrative and reach others like themselves.[23] Marginalized groups have the ability to insert themselves into stories previously dominated by the elite or the majority, sometimes historically and incorrectly giving rise to the idea that fanfiction and fan communities are part of a "deviant" culture. As online communities grow to include more than those readers who look or sound exactly like a canon character, fanfiction provides an outlet to create characters that these new audiences recognize.

Fan and fanfiction communities do not just rely on the original text to create the world that they fit into and enjoy; in many cases the world has already expanded to include adaptations in a media different from the original. In the case of Austen fandom, there are countless film and television adaptations, published (non-amateur) fanfiction such as *Mr. Darcy Takes a Wife*, and events or images that have entered the megaverse in such a way as to become practically canon. Moments such as Colin Firth undressing and diving into a pond (and then, wet and stoic, coming across Elizabeth Bennet) have entered the fan community as facts of the text (also known as "fan canon," or "fanon"), even though that moment never appears in the original *Pride and Prejudice*.[24]

Today fanfiction is more strictly defined as being a derivative story, written by a fan and shared openly and for free. Some fans balk at calling anything that is published or distributed for a profit fanfiction at all, situating much of what fans create and contribute in a gift economy.[25] The makeup of the community is also largely women and nonbinary people, and one could argue that the fact that communities who read and write fanfiction are largely comprised of the same actually contributes to the perpetuation of the idea that fanfiction should not be created for profit. When fic authors do publish their previously free work, fan communities can often retaliate. Fic writers have been shamed, called whores, and ostracized from fan communities for breaking the understood rules. This rhetoric, Jamison notes, follows a long tradition of shaming women for wanting pay for work that social norms say should be done out of love: child care, domestic work, and teaching, for example.[26] But for a community of writers who may otherwise find a path to traditional publishing challenging, fanfiction and the online communities around them offer an appealing alternative: a way to share their writing and their love of a story and characters with a group of people who value the same thing. The backlash against authors pulling fic to publish it for profit has not seemed to stir within the Austen fanfic communities, however. Many now-published fic authors have spoken of their experiences as fan writers as ones of unabashed support and encouragement, with fan readers being the ones to suggest that writers publish their work.

One example of a fanfiction turned novel is the *Fitzwilliam Darcy*, Gentleman series. At a signing in 2007, author Pamela Aidan discussed how the story progressed from labor-of-love to full-fledged trilogy published by Simon and Schuster. She recalled reading Austen fanfic on websites like the Republic of Pemberley and the Derbyshire Writers' Guild. When she couldn't find a story that detailed the events of *Pride and Prejudice* from Darcy's point of view, she decided to write her own.[27] Initially she only posted what later became the first novel, but once the readers fell in love with the story and asked for more, she continued the series. In response to fan requests that she publish a novel, Aidan sought out a self-publishing platform, and after the series became a sensation—Aidan was told that the series "sold more than any other self-published historical romance" at that time—she eventually agreed to an offer to have the series reprinted and distributed.[28]

Another Austen fanfic writer, Sharon Lathan, had a similar experience to Aidan's. On her website she shares the details of her journey from fanfic writer to published author.[29] Becoming a fan after seeing the 2005 film version of *Pride and Prejudice*, she plunged head first into fandom, consuming published media and free fanfic alike. When she couldn't find the story she wanted—details of the Darcys' post-wedding bliss—she decided to write her own. That led to a series, which garnered a devoted following of other fans, who encouraged her to self-publish, which eventually led to Sourcebooks, an independent publisher, picking up her series.[30] She now has three different *Pride and Prejudice* series in print: a prequel duology, a five-part sequel, and a trilogy of companion novels.[31]

Aidan's and Lathan's stories are examples of how the fanfiction community can create and support writers through less-than-traditional avenues to publishing. Aidan and Lathan did not start out wanting to professionally publish the next Austen spin-off, but because an enthusiastic, supportive audience of Austen fans offered feedback and encouragement, they were both able to launch a successful series. Fan writing communities all over do this: they essentially build writing groups around a common interest or text (like Austen), then share their time and talent both to help each other grow and to continue to enjoy this *thing* they all love in some way. In "Writing a New Text: The Role of Cyberculture in Fanfiction Writers' Transition to 'Legitimate' Publishing," Monica Flegel and Jenny Roth discuss how internet fan cultures have impacted fan writers who have made the jump to more traditional publishing routes.[32] They found, through interviews with fanfiction writers, that "the fanfiction community offers a crucial form of support and inspiration through audience reception and constructive criticism."[33]

Austen fandom, while not immune to infighting, has some benefits that make the process of publishing fan writing less problematic for other fans. With Austen's worlds and characters, for example, fan writers have the freedom of using novels long past their copyright expiration. This makes the

Austen megaverse ripe for novels, movies, television, and more because the need for licensing and permissions does not exist. There is no controlling authority on what is an Official Austen Product. Unlike fandoms where there may be officially licensed additions to a primary text (such as *Buffy the Vampire Slayer* getting an official line of comics after the run of the show ended), Austen fandom doesn't have someone controlling what gets produced or what doesn't. This makes the lines between "fanwork" and "published or original work" a lot harder to define, because the traditional authority that would create those boundaries (and potentially enforce them), is absent. Fans and for-profit media producers are free to take what they like, and do with it what they like. And if recent history is an indication, Austen fans are always thirsty for more stoic, awkward men in breeches and waistcoats attempting to woo feisty, forward-thinking heroines. This has led the Austen fandom to be fairly revolutionary in its ability to break the boundaries between fanfiction and for-profit publishing. The lack of clear lines makes it often hard to tell what, exactly, we mean when we say, "Jane Austen fanfiction." Are we talking about *only* stories available for free online? Do we include published novels that were traditional fanfiction at some point? Does the work of anyone who would call themselves an Austen fan—whether they have the money of a publisher or production studio behind them or not—count as "fan" work? The Austen fandom, and its lack of adherence to the traditional "rules" of fanfiction, make these questions much more complicated and, arguably, impossible to answer.

One thing is for sure, however: Austen fans have been rabid for more Jane for decades. Nothing seems to quell the desire; there will never be enough films, mashups, or erotic novels to satisfy the Janeite's obsession. We can attend balls and indulge in RPGs (role-playing games), buy Austen-themed tote bags and buttons, and read and reread her novels and letters endlessly, but we always come back to the original texts. This is where fanfiction can help fill an emotional void. Constance Grady explains that part of the enjoyment of fanfiction is because it gives fans a way to soothe the pain of a particularly difficult moment in a novel or television series, serves as a way to "outsource all [our] baser needs," and gives us the catharsis of a sentimental ending *in addition to* the emotional satisfaction found in reading the original text (emphasis in original).[34] While fanfiction cannot, and often does not intend, to replace the canon material, it does offer writers and readers a way to continue being emotionally present within a world they love, and find more ways to get the same emotional payoff that is received when reading an Austen novel. What if Elizabeth had not gone to Derbyshire but instead to the lakes, as they had originally planned? What if Willoughby had not been driven from Marianne by his need to marry rich? What if Henry Crawford had not run off with Maria Bertram?[35] How would these stories, these characters, have still found their due end? By changing details, small or large, we get to spend more time with characters and places we love, experiencing the joy we had that first time we picked up Austen and falling in love with them all over again. *This* is the allure of JAFF, *this* is why Austen spinoffs, adaptations, and reimaginings will continue to sell: because we all want to feel that way again. The first flush of feeling Darcy's eyes on Elizabeth during a ball. The desperation of Marianne running through a storm, heartbroken over Willoughby. The vindication of knowing Fanny was right to not trust Henry Crawford. Fanfiction offers us new ways to experience that rush, to get our Austen fix. And it is exciting because we think we know what is going to happen in the end, but we don't know *how* we are going to get there.

The world of Austen fanfiction specifically has grown in other ways, too: fic now exists in worlds beyond the original novels as the only source texts. Newer works that draw on Austen's novels, like *The Lizzie Bennet Diaries*, *Pride and Prejudice and Zombies*, and *Clueless* have their own fan spaces, their own fanfic, and their own fans. These additional Austen-related spheres can sometimes bring out questions and disagreements over "real" fans and if, for example, a fanfic set in the *Lizzie Bennet Diaries* world is Austen fanfic or—something else entirely. A quick scan through fanfiction.net's indexes reveals little consensus on these matters. A search for the keywords "lizzie bennet diaries" yields just over 300 stories, with the majority (265) tagged in the *Pride and Prejudice* world. However, 31 are tagged under the genre "web shows" (there is not a separate *LBD* tag), and the remaining are tagged under other book or television fandoms, which likely makes them "crossover" fics.[36] Additionally, one of the filters available under the *Pride and Prejudice* tag allows for stories to be sorted by "world." The options? BBC Miniseries, Book, *Lizzie Bennet Diaries*, Modern, Movie, or Regency. The options for where to place these stories that are fanfics-of-fanfics do not seem to offer up any definitive answers. *LBD* fic could reasonably be tagged as a web show, or as a *Pride and Prejudice* fic (and then further classified as "Lizzie Bennet Diaries," or "modern"). Either one could be equally correct. It makes parsing out the true extent of the Austen fanfic world a difficult task, and it creates a challenge for fans searching for fics to read, who may not think to look under "web series" when searching for *LBD* variations.

A similar search on Archive of Our Own reveals 1,019 fics. Unlike fanfiction .net, AO3 has a separate fandom tag for *LBD*, as well as options for "*Pride and Prejudice* and related fandoms" among others. While these allow for more granular tagging of stories, and makes it easier to categorize works into different areas, it doesn't necessarily alleviate the questions surrounding where these derivative fandoms fit within the larger Austen fan world, if they should be considered part of that fandom at all. The Austen fandom has simply become too big, with too many spinoffs and fanworks and subsections of subsections, that it would be near impossible to get fans to agree on a single, conclusive classification for all the different branches of Austen fanfiction that exist. An attempt to definitively categorize Austen fanfic would likely be unsuccessful, as individual preferences and ideas about what qualifies something as "Austen fanfic." (One story that we found throughout our digging inserted Austen characters into a Michigan J. Frog skit, where the only Austen-related content that remained were character names. Could one really call this Austen fanfic if it retains so few identifiable characteristics of the original text?)

With the rise of these new circles within the larger JAFF umbrella, it becomes even more difficult to categorize and delineate between different levels of writing and production on the large spectrum that is JAFF. Perhaps it doesn't matter all that much how we categorize or organize Austen fic. Austen fandom, and Austen fic, offer communities to those who want to write and read her works over and over. Perhaps what matters is that as it continues to exist at all, in spaces accessible by women, nonbinary individuals, and other underrepresented groups that continue to foster opportunities for writers to follow in Austen's literary footsteps, breaking and rewriting the rules as they go.

JAFF as Feminist Practice

As much as there are fans supporting other fans, there can also be fighting (sometimes called "fan wank"[37]), shaming, hate trolling, and all the other nasty things that can crop up online where identities can be anonymous. Fan spaces are not immune to the general hate that can sometimes seem to take over internet interactions. These disagreements can crop up for a variety of reasons: dissent about the source text, arguments over text interpretation, intolerance for certain viewpoints, even "ship wars."[38] For some fans, it can often be enough to drive them away from the fandom. This type of dissent is seen most often in contemporary fandoms: fans of television, films, or novels that are much more current than Austen, as well as ones that tend to still be producing official canon content. As mentioned before, the lack of an official creator of Austen-related content makes it a lot more open for fans and film producers alike to make their own interpretations and create new content. That is not to say that Austen fandom is immune to disagreements between fans, but especially when it comes to fanfiction, many of the most popular hosting platforms for Austen fanfic are much more moderated (read: moderated at all) than other fan spaces. These moderated spaces tend to have more regulations and policies in place for dealing with inappropriate or hateful interaction and people who often volunteer their labor to maintain the forum's standards and procedures.[39] Regardless, the space for writers to interact over the texts, fanfic or canon, still exists, and it allows women, as Rachel Crouch explains, "to tell stories wholly through the female gaze"—something that in any other type of medium is rarely possible.

A common plot found among fanfiction, and JAFF is certainly no exception, is the romance. And while that may seem counter to feminism for some, the truth is that romance writing is one of the few arenas, other than fanfiction, where women's voices reign and the female gaze is prioritized. It makes sense, then, that these two types of writing would coincide. Henry Jenkins also notes that research has shown that female readers tend to focus more on relationships and characters than do male readers, and are generally more open to deconstructing and playing with existing stories.[40] He is speaking specifically of *Star Trek* fanfiction in this case, noting that the largely women-centered fic writers took the "space opera" format of the original series and turned to the formulas of soaps and romances in order to explore character relationships in a more mature, realistic fashion.[41] While Austen's original novels are obviously not space operas in form, her novels are extensively character- and relationship-driven, so it makes sense that readers would continue the stories, or invent new ones with existing characters, in a format that prizes the female gaze that Austen also prioritizes (i.e., the romance).

While we were able to enjoy a few nonromantic fics, it was clear from diving into the deep end of Austen fanfic that of the stories most fans want to read and write there is the romance (including racy, erotic, sex-insert stories). And there is absolutely nothing wrong with wanting to read great, romantic stories, or wanting to read different variations of your OTP[42] falling in love, over and over again, despite whatever obstacles may be put in front of them. In romance novels women's desires are at the forefront. Women are intelligent, fierce, and independent heroes of their own stories—in both romance novels and in Austen, truly—so the blend of these two spaces makes for an amazing space for women writers to do what they want with characters that they love.

Part of the joy of reading this particular plot in fanfiction, in addition to original romance, is that we *know* the ending that's coming. We know that Elinor and Edward will somehow find their way to each other. We know that Elizabeth and Darcy will overcome their animosity and fall deeply in love. We know that Edmund will someday come to recognize Fanny's quiet love for him.[43] Even if a canon pairing isn't what someone is looking for, they can use the internal tagging system and summaries offered by writers to find a romantic pairing they *do* want to read—whether it be Elizabeth/Charlotte, Elizabeth/Wickham, or Elizabeth/Colonel Fitzwilliam. If wanting to experience the journey of falling in love along with your favorite characters drives someone to read or write fanfic, then the good news is that the Austen fandom is well supplied with witty, talented writers to satisfy the craving, regardless of who is doing the falling. Lev Grossman argues that fandom and fan writing is "inherently inclusive" and where fans will find "every race, nationality, ethnicity, language, religion, age, and sexual orientation represented."[44] This type of inclusivity is important to feminism—whose very existence is about creating equality—which makes Austen fanfic communities an intersection of so many areas (Austen's novels, romance novels, and fanfiction) where women's voices are prioritized, a uniquely feminist space. Grossman continues by noting that the fans will often spend comparable time being friends, getting to know each other, and supporting fellow fans as they do focusing on the reading and writing.[45]

The interaction between readers and writers was basically built into the foundation of fanfic communities from the beginning, perhaps due in part to its historical operation as a gift economy. It involves authors talking to each other and talking to their readers. It involves readers talking to authors, and talking to each other. These exchanges build a community that becomes about more than just the fic. Often fans begin to feel like they know each other, and they build friendships that transcend the fandom. For the writers, fanfic can fill multiple needs, even outside the immediate desire to contribute to a fandom they love or right a wrong in a story. Writing can be an outlet for stress, a way to relieve anxiety, an avenue for dealing with emotions otherwise too difficult to confront (and we say this as writers ourselves). Some professional authors write fanfic for fun and turn to it during times of writer's block. The stakes are not as high, the pressure off. S. E. Hinton is one well-known example of a novel writer who also participates in fanfiction.[46] Writing fanfic is as much about writing *for yourself*, perhaps even more so, than it is writing for other fans. Sometimes writing for the sake of writing is exactly the point, and fanfiction provides the setting, character, and plot twist. All the writer has to do is fill in the gaps.

In addition to fulfilling a personal need, the community that builds up around fanfic can also provide external validation for those who participate. External validation could come as likes and comments on a fic—validation of the work itself—but also outside of a fic. It is not unusual for a fanfic writer on Tumblr, for example, to also share personal posts about their lives: good experiences, difficulties in their lives, political perspectives. As fans, we have seen fanfic writers who come out as queer to their readers before they tell anyone else in their lives or who share stories about meeting a potential romantic partner, or even seemingly innocuous things like sharing book recommendations or playing "Ask Me Anything" games with followers. Many times, especially when sharing difficulties in their lives, readers—fellow fans they may never meet in their lifetime—will flood their pages with well wishes, prayers, compliments, virtual hugs, and other encouragement. They support each other not just as fans and content creators or consumers but the same as they would a friend in their physical world. Fanfic has created a space for budding writers, yes, but also for women to support each other through, well, life. This furthers the feminist work being done in fanfiction spaces: women supporting other women through personal and professional strife, building communities of safety and care when they may not find these things in their daily lives offline.

This type of fan support can be fickle, though. One of the most controversial practices in fandom is when authors will pull their fic, revise it (or not), and publish it as an original novel. The phenomenon of fanfiction-to-publication is not isolated to the Jane Austen fan community, and although the earlier examples of Pamela Aidan and Sharon Lathan's experiences were largely positive, many fanfic-turned-published authors do not have as enthusiastic an experience as theirs. There has long been debate in fandom over whether or not writers should monetize their works, and the reasons against are not always as simple as they might seem. One obvious push against the sale of fanfiction is that writers are dealing with someone else's creative property.[47] A less obvious objection many fans have is simply that the genre has historically operated as a gift economy, and many believe it should not operate on a for-profit model. This can be complicated by the fact that it is not always *only* the fic's author who puts work into a story being written and shared. Many writers and fic communities use beta readers, or other fans who do not write themselves, but work as unpaid editors to give feedback, help with revisions, and otherwise polish up a story before an author posts it online. When authors who have used beta readers then pull their fic and publish it, people, fellow fans, who have put time, expertise, and work into a story often get no credit—and no compensation.

Backlash against authors who use their place in a fandom to build a market for publishing their work can be considerable; fanfiction writers, especially good ones, are generally well known in their respective fan areas. E. L. James, author of the *50 Shades of Grey* trilogy, experienced this when she pulled her *Twilight* fanfiction, "Master of the Universe," to revise and publish under the new title.[48] The author received significant adverse reactions from the *Twilight* fans, and some big-name fic writers, who knew her history in fanfiction. Some of these fans likened her choice to "pull and publish" to prostitution and accused her of exploiting her "fandom cred" in order to build a successful franchise.[49]

As it turns out, Aidan and Lathan's experiences are the exception, and James's experience, Flegal and Roth found, is much more the rule in many fan spaces.[50] Regardless of resistance to a for-profit model among many fanfic writers, the genre seems to be moving in that direction. Amazon.com has launched a platform called *Kindle Worlds* that allows content creators to publish fic in existing "worlds"—and under official licenses. Only a small number of licenses are available at the moment, but Amazon promises more on the way.[51] If fans don't start to monetize their work, as Abigail De Kosnik discusses in "Should Fan Fiction Be Free?," someone else will recognize the opportunity for profit and fans will not be the ones to principally benefit from their labor.[52] In addition to publishing fanfiction at a profit, there is also a history of writers pulling to publish, changing details that mark a text within a certain world. This is what E. L. James did with her *Twilight* fic turned *50 Shades of Grey*. As discussed before, though, this practice is not relegated to fans in the last few decades. The history of literature is writers ripping off others' stories and reinventing them.

Common assumptions about fanfiction writers and readers is that they are almost always, without exception, women, or identify as such. Similarly, common assumptions about Austen readers and fans are that they are also almost always, without exception, women or woman-identifying.[53] Deborah Yaffe found during her exploration into Janeite culture that the assumption about fans' gender, at least, was based somewhat in reality.[54] Fanfiction writing especially has long been a haven for women and nonbinary individuals, mostly because they have been kept out of traditional circles.[55] Women writers have responded to this exclusion, in a sense, by going underground. The first fan communities (also majority women) published and shared their work via snail mail and zines shared at conventions, but now they are able to share using websites and blogging platforms. It makes sense then that these women-driven spheres of writing and fandom would collide to create an ideal space for women to write, share, criticize, and publish. Jane Austen was arguably a feminist before feminism was even a thing, and now her fans are using the stories and characters she provided to continue to support (emotionally and monetarily) other women writers. I like to think Jane would be proud of this legacy of women supporting women, seeing as she strived to support herself through writing, and was bitingly critical of those who discounted women's contributions to society.

Whether or not every Austen fan and scholar can agree on whether or not Austen and her writing were feminist, it would be difficult to argue that her *legacy* is not feminist. Women today are writing their stories—because of Austen. Women today are supporting other women writers—because of Austen. Women today are refusing to accept mainstream media's dismissal of the value of a woman's gaze—because of Austen. Austen-related fanfiction, by nature of its very existence, is a feminist practice.

4

You're Only a Secondary Character If You Let Yourself Be: Lydia Bennet, Fans, and Feminism

ZOE & HOLLY

"It is a truth universally acknowledged that nothing gets done without alcohol."
—aquackingduck, paraphrasing Lydia in *The Lizzie Bennet Diaries*, via Tumblr

Adapting Regency novels, or anything old, into a modern context can be really difficult, and when it comes to Austen there are few standout examples. *Clueless*, of course, takes the cake when it comes to film modernizations, but YouTube has provided a platform for the tiny silver screen to shine. *The Lizzie Bennet Diaries*, produced by Pemberley Digital, is a YouTube web series[1] that that ran from 2012 to 2013. *LBD* tells the modern-day story of Lizzie Bennet, a twenty-four-year-old graduate student who lives at home with her parents and two sisters and who vlogs[2] about her life. The typical cast of *Pride and Prejudice* populates the vlog series: Lizzie's older sister, Jane, who works in fashion and is burdened by student loan debt; younger sister Lydia, a community college student obsessed with boys and parties; and best friend Charlotte, who attends graduate school with Lizzie. This modern take transports Austen's characters into a world where women are faced with school, student loans, low-paying jobs, beginning careers, and adulthood without leaving the nest rather than being faced only with the choice of a marriage partner.

So how does a modernization of *Pride and Prejudice* make itself different than just placing the characters in modern day? One of the most interesting changes to the world of *Pride and Prejudice* in this updated version is how the story choses to treat the character of Lydia Bennet. In *PP*, Lydia has very little direct communication with either Elizabeth or Jane. While she may be present or in the same room, she rarely directly converses with either of the two eldest Bennets. Instead, her presence or actions are often simply noted. Plus, because the storyline follows Elizabeth when she is absent from home, large portions of the canon novel do not include Lydia at all. *LBD* has other ideas: Lydia's character in *LBD* has much more interaction with her sisters, cares about their approval, and keeps herself in the story through her own vlogs and her use of social media. As a transmedia project, fan interaction with Lydia and her various social media platforms also allows viewers to be not just consumers but participants in her story. We're going to take a look at the fan interaction with Lydia's character in *LBD* and see how it demonstrates a remarkably different reaction to this modern Lydia compared to her novel counterpart. In *PP* Lydia is an often-disliked obstacle to Elizabeth and Darcy's happy ending and serves only as a foil to her eldest sisters. In *LBD* she is integral to Elizabeth's own emotional maturation and revelations, and many fans, most often women, are drawn to her character and demanded more Lydia—so much more that in response to fan reaction, two writers from the series penned a follow-up novel specifically about Lydia's life post-vlog.

Lydia is first introduced in *LBD* as part of Lizzie's videos and she begins the web series much the same as she does in the novel: she loves parties, boys, and doesn't take life too seriously. In fact, in just the first five videos of *LBD*, Lizzie describes Lydia multiple times as slutty and irresponsible. In episode 2 (*LBD*, "My Sisters: Problematic to Practically Perfect") Lizzie characterizes Lydia as a "stupid, whorey slut," says she is the most likely of the three sisters to end up an alcoholic or drug addict, and likens her to a destructive puppy. Not only that, but all of Lydia's appearances in the first few episodes of *LBD* involve her doing nothing more than excitedly acting as the gossip transmitter, sharing the details of the new neighbor, Bing Lee. She gleefully relates how rich, single, and attractive he is, such as in episode 4 ("Bing Lee and His 500 Teenage Prostitutes"), where she tells Lizzie about the guests Bing is bringing to an upcoming wedding: his sister Caroline and an attractive, rich friend of Bing's who is also in town (William Darcy). Even her wardrobe in the earlier episodes of *LBD* play into the expected Lydia character: she wears bright colors, short skirts, red lipstick, and eye-catching jewelry. It is clear from the first few episodes that this Lydia is just as flighty and materialistic as her canon counterpart.

Until episode 28 of *LBD* ("Meeting Bing Lee") Lydia appears only in Lizzie's videos, most often to help with reenactments of events that have happened in Lizzie's life for the camera, and as Lydia often reminds the viewers, to bring the "adorbs."[3] Her character continues without much variation as being obsessed with parties, boys, and gossip, exemplified in episode 20 ("Enjoy the Adorbs"), when she hijacks Lizzie's video and shares her own plan to get Jane and Bing together: "Bing will host a party. He and Jane will get drunk. Drunken hookup. Marriage." But during these first videos Lydia is dependent on Lizzie for fame and a camera, and as the series progresses, Lizzie occasionally leaves the family home. It is during these times that Lydia records her own vlog to share, and as Lydia's story splits from Lizzie's, we are going to talk about how Pemberley Digital's storytelling departs from a twenty-first-century adaptation into the blurry realm of transformational fanfiction.

Lydia's vlog, titled *The Lydia Bennet*[4] (here, *Lydia*), is entirely optional for viewers; it was not linked on the main YouTube channel but instead had its own channel. Lydia's story eventually reconnected with Lizzie's and the rest of the canon cast, but her side story was exactly that. Viewers of the show got the opportunity to see Lydia's perspective on the main events of *LBD* as well as additional stories about Lydia's life and friends. The vlog begins with typical Lydia: self-absorbed and materialistic. She shares short snippets of her life, such as the first episode ("Boredom"), shot while she is visiting her cousin Mary, whom she makes fun of for enjoying reading and not expressing emotions. Later, in *Lydia*'s episode 3 ("The Lodger"), she admits to renting out her cousin's attic to a complete stranger in order to make some extra money. As with her early appearances in *LBD*, the first episodes of *Lydia* perpetuate the depiction of Lydia from *Pride and Prejudice*: unintelligent, annoying, and self-absorbed. However, Lydia's personal vlog becomes important for her character development when it begins to deviate from the original canon depiction. Lydia has a falling out with her sisters and cousin Mary (shown in *LBD* episodes 73 and 74, and in *Lydia* episodes 17 and 18) over her perceived irresponsibility, and she consequently turns to George Wickham for comfort. Filling in the story that is left dark in *Pride and Prejudice* and on Lizzie's main channel in *LBD*, viewers are able to watch Lydia's mistakes in tandem with the rest of the *LBD* story, and we see the choices that eventually lead to her "scandal." By showing these hidden moments from Lydia's perspective, the series is able to shift Lydia from a hopeless flirt who is punished for her lack of sense of propriety to the sympathetic victim of a manipulative man.

The team at Pemberley Digital also sought to bring fans into the narrative throughout the entire process; each main character had a Twitter account, while select characters used other platforms to share photos or additional character-building details, such as a fashion lookbook for Jane Bennet. Characters even addressed fans' comments and questions in the storyline, most notably through Q&A videos. These additional platforms allowed fans to interact with Lydia in "real time" and allowed the creative team behind the series to respond to the fan reaction to her, which was largely positive and empathetic. Lori Halvorsen Zerne describes the show's ability to create sympathy for Lydia as "a feat that Austen does not even attempt."[5] Through transmedia and fanfiction, Lydia is no longer only a foil to Elizabeth's good sense and manners—she is allowed the space to learn, grow, and develop as the star of her own story. In much of the criticism surrounding *Pride and Prejudice*, it is Elizabeth and her relationship with Darcy that is dissected and discussed, but Zerne notes that much of the commentary around *The Lizzie Bennet Diaries* has "centered on Lydia Bennet's storyline in the series."[6] With *LBD* and the companion *Lydia* videos, and with transmedia adding depth and layers to her character not available in the canon, Lydia Bennet is no longer relegated to the status of secondary character, and fans flocked to her as a relatable, sympathetic person, rather than just Elizabeth's annoying, flighty little sister.

Much criticism of *Pride and Prejudice* has centered on how Lydia, among other characters, is written to represent various stages of development and how she in particular is presented as a foil to the growth and maturation of Elizabeth and Darcy. Alan Goldman argues in *Philosophy and the Novel* that the characters progress through various stages of moral development; he argues that Lydia represents one stage of "stunted moral development."[7] Goldman's analysis of Lydia's character, as "all self-centered emotion and completely lacking in judgment" and as having not reached the stage of recognizing social conventions, holds true for *LBD!*Lydia[8] at the beginning of the series.[9] However, it does not bear out in the end, as the character has progressed through various stages of development and ends the web series as a more mature character than when she started—which further pushes this adaptation into fanfiction. Much of this growth happens because of two distinct relationships: with her sisters and with George Wickham.

Lydia's main companion in the canon *Pride and Prejudice* is the sister closest to her in age, Catherine, called Kitty. Lydia never takes Elizabeth and Jane into her confidence the way she does Kitty, as evidenced by the letters Kitty receives while Lydia is away at Brighton and by the fact that she is less surprised than the rest of the family when Lydia runs off with Wickham.[10] In *LBD*, the number of Bennet sisters is cut from five to three, with Kitty becoming an *actual* cat, and Mary becoming a cousin. Removing Lydia's main confidant changes the dynamic between her and her elder sisters; it is established early in *LBD* that Lizzie is closer to Jane, by reason of age and more similar personalities, and that Lydia can sometimes feel like an outsider in her own family. In the second video of the main series, "Problematic to Practically Perfect," Lizzie describes her relationship with Jane: "We're super close. She's practically my best friend." On the other hand, she likens Lydia to a misbehaving puppy. In a later episode Lizzie refers to Jane as her "second best-est friend ever" (second to Charlotte), and when Jane questions why she is second best, Lizzie replies, "Oh just be glad you aren't Lydia. She doesn't even rank" (*LBD* episode 12, "Jane Chimes In"). It is possible, even likely, that this is said in jest, but it is only one example among many of the different ways Lizzie dismisses Lydia as not being as important to her as Jane or Charlotte.

Despite feeling like a third wheel to smart Lizzie and perfect Jane, it is clear from the beginning that Lydia seeks the love and acceptance of her older sisters. Lydia wants to be included in her sisters' lives, as evidenced in *Lydia* episodes 12–15, when she runs away to Los Angeles to visit Jane, who has recently taken a new job. In contrast, Lydia in *Pride and Prejudice* at no point displays a desire to be closer to Elizabeth and Jane, only talking to them directly to gossip about the goings-on of the officers quartering at Meryton, to express her wild disappointment at being denied the things she wants, or to ask for money.

Perhaps the most important representation of how much *LBD*!Lydia's sisters' approval means to her is shown in *LBD* episode 73 ("2+1"), where Lizzie gifts Lydia her birthday presents. One is a necklace and the other a book titled, *Where Did I Park My Car? A Party Girl's Guide to Becoming a Successful Adult*. At first Lydia laughs, treating it as a joke, but when Lizzie corrects her and explains that it is a real gift, and that she means it sincerely, Lydia is immediately hurt. She views this gift as a rejection by her sister of who she is as a person—that who she is isn't enough. Also of note in this episode is that Lydia accuses Lizzie of "taking Darcy's side" instead of hers, implying that she wants to rank above Darcy in Lizzie's eyes, something that never would have occurred to the canon!Lydia, who only sees dollar signs and boring manners when she looks at Mr. Darcy. In the episode the Darcy comment is a quick exchange, but an important one in terms of the relationship between these two characters. In contrast to the novel, where Elizabeth and Lydia hardly interact, in *LBD* Lizzie is one of the most important people in Lydia's life and vice versa; this rejection hurts Lydia so deeply that it makes her susceptible to the manipulation of George Wickham. This is never more clear than in the final *Lydia* episode, "Good Enough," where she explains why she loves George: "He's so . . . good . . . to me. He treats me like I'm someone, I guess, um, he always puts me first and I didn't know people really did that." She goes on to compare her family relationships to her relationship with George, noting that she thought she could always count on her family but has learned that they might not always be around, and she contrasts that realization with being "chosen" by Wickham. About halfway through the video, she looks directly at the camera and says, "I feel good enough for somebody for once." After feeling rejected by her sisters, not good enough for her parents, and not wanted by her cousin Mary,[11] she turns to the one person who appears to love and support her for who she is. Adding more depth and dimension to the familial relationships in Lydia's life makes her more relatable and sympathetic, right from the beginning of the series, and provides the catalyst for Lydia's growth and development as a character, allowing her to continue to hold the audience's sympathy despite her mistakes.

In Austen's novel, Lydia is hardly heard from again following her marriage to Wickham. While other characters make reference to her or her recent marriage, the character herself does not reappear and only communicates with Elizabeth once, in a letter she sends upon Elizabeth's marriage to Darcy, asking for money.[12] *LBD* deviates from this completely, not only featuring Lydia again in the vlogs—albeit a much more subdued, quiet version of the boun-cy, flamboyant Lydia who appeared in the early videos—but also making the repairing of her relationship with Lizzie one of the main story arcs of the final videos and ending the story with Lydia no longer in a relationship with Wick-ham. The fans also went on an emotional journey with Lydia, as evidenced by the interaction with her Twitter account and the comments on the YouTube videos. The tweets "liked" by Lydia's Twitter account (@TheLydiaBennet) fol-lowing her New Year's adventure in Vegas ranged from shaming and chastising Lydia for her relationship with George—and in some cases blaming her for his manipulation—to defending Lydia to Lizzie. On Tumblr, one fan even wrote Lydia a heartfelt letter to reassure and comfort her following George's betray-al.[13] In *LBD* Lydia is more than just a foil to Lizzie. She is her own character, al-lowed to learn and grow from her mistakes, and the fans loved her for it.

The relationship between Lydia and Wickham is one of the major changes to Lydia's character. It defines her "downfall," instigates a reconciliation with her sisters, and invites fan reactions and criticisms regarding the changes. For the Lydia in *PP*, the marriage with Wickham is a success. Although Wickham, like Willoughby and others before him, is a typical Austen rake, Lydia manag-es to get what she wants: Wickham has a position in society; he's incredibly attractive; and she marries before any of her sisters, giving her superiority over them. *Pride and Prejudice* isolates the reader from the terror of the rake; for canon!Lydia, the rogue's manipulation ends favorably for her.[14] *LBD*!Lydia, on the other hand, draws the short straw. While canon!Lydia's choices give her a newfound freedom, *LBD*!Lydia's choices are taken away from her.

Rather than willingly run off with, and eventually marry, Wickham, Lydia finds herself pushed further and further from her friends and family that she wants to stay close to. In some ways this is her own fault,[15] but it's also true that her support network is slowly crumbling around her. Lydia runs to Las Vegas for her twenty-first birthday, gets into some kind of (unnamed) trouble, and Wickham rescues her. They begin to date, and Wickham works to manip-ulate Lydia; he uses her newfound internet fame, their relationship, and the fact that Lydia's sisters haven't reached out to make her even more vulnerable before finally convincing her to (consensually) film themselves having sex. (It's strongly implied that this is the first time the two are having sex together.) Although Lydia agrees to the filming, she doesn't know that he plans to release it online. He uses the fan base he's helped build through his participation on her videos to create anticipation for a countdown website of his own entitled "See YouTube star Lydia Bennet reveal EVERYTHING."[16] Lydia comes home one day to find Lizzie yelling at her, only to discover the website then and there.

Lydia's character can be difficult to modernize, as her "shame" of running off with, ostensibly, a party boy might make her family frustrated, but the shame aspects don't apply in the same way today because elopement and premarital sex do not carry the same stigmas as they once did. The producers and writers at Pemberley Digital instead took a completely different direction. By taking away Lydia's choice, she becomes both a more vulnerable figure and a completely different character than that of her canon counterpart. She becomes fanfiction.

In many ways fanfiction gives voices to the voiceless, including underrepresented populations, and in this case victims of partner manipulation and harassment.[17, 18] For Lydia, her lack of choice creates a situation that many modern women, sadly, can relate to. George's character, one we don't get to see in such depth in the canon material, is narrowed from the general party boy the audience met when he was with Lizzie to a manipulative and dangerous partner for Lydia. Pemberley Digital's use of transmedia storytelling gives the audience multiple ways to watch Lydia's fanfictionization and her collapse.

After Lydia's fight with Lizzie, in which Lizzie attempts to push Lydia into growing up and being more mature, Lydia heads to Vegas for her birthday (this is the *LBD* version of Lydia traveling to Brighton). Because she was not featured on the main vlog during this time, the transmedia team at Pemberley Digital kept her Twitter feed updated regularly. Lydia's tweets combined with her video "Vegas, Bitches!!" begin mundanely enough: Lydia is very excited to get drunk and party. But soon her Twitter feed, and even the next video update just a few hours later ("Midnight"), changes tone. These tweets, combined with the following videos, give a fuller picture of Lydia's mental state.[19]

The transmedia that so brilliantly defined *LBD* showed *LBD*!Lydia's descent into depression and low self-esteem. In *Pride and Prejudice* Lydia is overwhelmed with joy to be among the officers in the north, and once she marries Wickham, she becomes even happier. In the 1995 BBC miniseries adaptation Lydia and Wickham are shown living together (and implied to be having premarital sex) while in London, but Lydia shows no indication of depression, worry, or self-harm. In the 2005 adaptation Lydia not only brags about her new romance but gloats repeatedly at the dinner table. These glimpses into Lydia's state of mind in other adaptations are not in the original text, but show Lydia's interactions with Wickham in a positive light.[20] Yet in *LBD*, as soon as Lydia returns from Vegas, she does not seem to be entirely her usual bouncy self (*Lydia* episode 22, "Surprise!"). She becomes quiet and unsure when talking about George, whereas canon!Lydia would be bragging all over town. Additionally, Lydia's wardrobe during her relationship with George differs from her usual flamboyant choices. She wears mostly greys, occasionally white, very little makeup, and minimal jewelry rather than her hot pinks and showy necklaces. Every part of her personality is toned down.

Just a few videos after "Surprise," and still with a silent Twitter feed, the audience finally gets a solid glimpse of both Lydia's state of mind and George's ability to manipulate her. In the video "Strangers," Lydia jokes that she is hanging out with George over "everyone's better judgment," to which he replies, "After what I did for you in Vegas?!" Although the audience is never privy to the details of Lydia's adventures in Vegas, Lydia's response indicates that George must have done her a large favor. Her entire demeanor changes from what might be seen as "old Lydia" (bubbly, fun, joking), to demure and submissive. She immediately apologizes as though she has deeply offended him, and although George says that he was only joking, the pause between Lydia's apology and George's "joke" feels too long. Combined with his smile at Lydia's sudden change of character, the entire section of the episode makes for a very uncomfortable watch.[21]

These major changes to Lydia's storyline—her fanfictionization—are deeply tied to the victimization of her character. Although the manipulation and potential abuse complicate the character, giving her layers and eventually strength, some fans took issue with the fact that a modernized version of Lydia has less power over her own fate than the version from the 1790s. One article, from the Carnegie Mellon student newspaper the *Tartan*, argues that

Lydia's "shame" moments in *Pride and Prejudice* and *LBD*[22] are not analogous.[23] In the original text Lydia chose to run away with Wickham, and in the article writer Chloe Thompson explains that "Lydia at least had agency in the novel. . . . When a woman in a novel written in 1813 has more agency than a woman in a web series created in 2012, you have a problem."[24] In the original novel the shame—and choice—is Lydia's, but it mostly affects her family; it affects Lizzie, from whose point of view the story derives its central conflict. Lydia's choice in the matter, that she decided to run away, shows a blatant disregard for the societal norms and her family's well-being, and that choice actually makes canon!Lydia incredibly feminist: she unapologetically sought personal and sexual gratification. Yet, as Zerne writes, blaming Lydia's lack of choice in *LBD* on her is another way of victim blaming: "Lydia's story demonstrates that even with greater sexual freedom and equality, women remain vulnerable to unscrupulous men."[25] In today's world, following the #MeToo movement on Twitter and other platforms, it's even more important to look back just a few years and see this web series as important. Although we don't see Lydia sexually abused or assaulted, the clues are left to show that she was, at the least, emotionally manipulated, and that she later was sexually assaulted by the threatened nonconsensual release of a sex tape. The balance of power that George pushes by constantly mentioning what he did for Lydia in Vegas, the fact that he's all she has, demeaning the relationship with her sisters—these are all classic abuse tactics and because Lydia is on the inside, vulnerable, and has no one to turn to (which is by George's design) by the time she (and to some degree the audience) realizes the extent of George's manipulation, she has been broken down completely.[26] They've changed the nature of Lydia's "shame" to one that shows the depravity of George Wickham and the way that anyone, even a smart, savvy, bubbly young woman from a middle-class family, can be abused or sexually harassed. It's not her fault and never was. Wickham took advantage of her and abused her for fun—and profit.

The website "set up by George Wickham," lydiabennettape.com, actually existed during the live run of the show but no longer does, and is one of the few pieces of the transmedia story to be wiped from existence *within* the story.[27] While fans could theoretically match up dates and times of YouTube videos to tweets and Tumblr posts, this website was an in-world transmedia experience that could only happen in real time. After all, Darcy purchases the company that owns the domain and removes the site, and so the audience witnessed the countdown clock stop and then the website disappear.

Lydia's "shame" in both *LBD* and *Pride and Prejudice* are based, at least in part, on the sexual nature of the relationship between Lydia and Wickham. Considering Lizzie's comments in early videos referring to Lydia as a slut or whore,[28] there is a strong implication that Lydia sleeps around. Certainly canon!Lydia would not be a virgin if she were mapped directly onto modern life—her "indiscretions" in pre-Victorian England, given her penchant for teasing the officers, would be of a sexual nature.[29] Yet the major manipulation, abuse, and collapse of Lydia's self in *LBD* revolves around sex and consent, but not in a promiscuous way. In the *Lydia* video "Kicks" (episode 25) Lydia explains to George that Brent (a character mentioned in one of her previous videos) had spread rumors about her that were untrue but that people believed them anyway, with the implication that the rumors were about Lydia sleeping around. In the following video (episode 26, "Dreams"), George says, "You and I haven't even . . . anyways . . ." implying that Lydia and George have not yet had sex. And possibly most important, when Lydia and George do have sex, he (consensually) films them, and then (nonconsensually) advertises the sex tape on the internet, using the internet fame that he fanned without Lydia knowing while emotionally abusing her in front of her vlog audience. George's final manipulation, the threatened sex tape release, is of an entirely sexual nature—just as the Bennet family worries that canon!Lydia is living in sin.[30] In *LBD* Lydia does care, whereas in *Pride and Prejudice* she seems unaware and uncaring about the nature of her "crime." In fact, in many portrayals of canon!Lydia in film, she is presented as *proud* of her conquest, something that women are still shamed for today.

Lydia is put in a terrible position in this version of her story. Yes, the story ends positively, and with therapy, but Lydia's journey is unpleasant and uncomfortable to watch, and it could be triggering to relate to. When Lydia and Lizzie finally reconnect, it's Lizzie who confronts Lydia about the sex tape (*LBD* "Consequences," episode 85), which is also how Lydia learns of its public nature. She is devastated, insisting that George, who promised that he loved her, would not do such a terrible act. Lydia simply cannot accept that what, for her, was an act of love, could be manipulated into a bid for money and power: "He would never . . . he loves me." In the following video with Lydia ("An Understanding," episode 86), she admits that her own videos "catalogue a car crash," and she tells Lizzie that she blames herself for her misdeeds. Lydia insists that she, rather than George, is at fault for the sexual manipulation, telling Lizzie, "None of this would have happened if I hadn't been acting like a stupid, whorey slut again, right?" and "I let him film us having sex, Lizzie, I let him do that . . . I said it was okay." These abuse and PTSD symptoms are the result of Wickham's targeted and scripted manipulation in their relationship, which Lydia finally understands as she tearfully tells Lizzie, "He said that I didn't love him as much as he loved me and I needed to prove it. So I said okay. So that he wouldn't leave." Lizzie does not judge her sister for trusting George, just as the audience shouldn't; that she was able to be manipulated is not a reflection on Lydia, her judgment, her character, or her virtue.[31] All these revelations—of Lydia's state of mind, the extent of George's manipulations and abuse, a full reconnection with Lizzie, and that Lydia, despite all of this, still loves George—comes in a difficult-to-watch five minutes and twenty-seven seconds of episode 86.

In *LBD* the story moves from being all about Lizzie as she discovers that she no longer knows her own sister, to being about Lizzie and Lydia, as the big moment of final development for both women comes at the same time. Lydia, no longer the naïve and bubbly girl the viewers first encountered, is a victim of sexual harassment, partner abuse, and internet fraud, but she has returned to her sisters, and they love her no matter what. This resolution, this chance to be self-reflective and grow as a character, is an opportunity that is not given to canon!Lydia, who is simply married off to Wickham and shipped north. In canon she is removed as an obstacle to Elizabeth and Darcy's marriage. In *LBD* she is integral to Lizzie's own character growth and story resolution. And while there were certainly a large number of viewers who watched the series in anticipation of Lizzie and Darcy's relationship, there were also a significant number (these authors included) who were cheering for Lydia to get the redemption and resolution she deserved. In a way, *LBD* gave *Pride and Prejudice* an alternate love story to root for: the sisterly love between Lydia and Lizzie. This is even emphasized by the fact that while Lizzie and Darcy do get their on-screen resolution, the final video ("The End," episode 100) does not feature Darcy at all. Instead, appearing alongside Lizzie are best friend Charlotte and little sister Lydia. Lydia drops her much-loved catchphrase ("Whaaaaat!"), and we see the two sisters embrace and make plans to spend time together. *LBD* began and ended as a woman's narrative, told by women, and focused on issues other than romance that face modern women: education, careers, and friendship. While some of the choices made by Pemberley Digital may have taken away some of Lydia's agency, in the arc of the story itself, the decision to allow Lydia a resolution that did not include being married off to a cad, and the focus on the friendships between the female characters in addition to the romantic relationships, *The Lizzie Bennet Diaries* reinforces that this was a story by women, about women, and for women.

Following the final vlog episode, the world of *LBD* saw many companion projects from producers and fans alike: a kickstarter for a DVD boxed set, two books, Internet memes, and even fanfiction set within the world of *LBD*.[32] Of the follow-up projects to *LBD*, the most interesting was the decision to write *The Epic Adventures of Lydia Bennet*, a novel that details Lydia's life after the end of Lizzie's story. The novel follows Lydia as she attempts to move past her internet infamy, figure out a path for her life, and come to terms with Wickham's abuse and betrayal. The authors of the novel have credited the fan reaction to Lydia's character as the catalyst for writing the sequel. The book's acknowledgements begin by saying, "*The Epic Adventures of Lydia Bennet* is the direct result of people caring about a secondary character so much, she needed the chance to tell her own story. Thus, everyone who tweeted, Tumblr-posted, or said anything about how much Lydia's story meant to them is the reason this book exists."[33] They also extend credit to the actress who portrayed Lydia in *LBD*, Mary Kate Wiles, for bringing her to life and redeeming "a character that most people dislike in *Pride and Prejudice*."[34] The fanfictionization of Lydia's story, and the fans' rabid interactions with the character during the run of the series and after, succeeded in encouraging Pemberley Digital to create more content and allowed fans more space and time with a character they had grown to love.

5

Subverting the Stereotype: Representation in Austen Fanon

HOLLY

Canon: brown eyes, frizzy hair and very clever. White skin was never specified. Rowling loves black Hermione.

—J. K. Rowling, via Twitter

In 2015, casting for the new play *Harry Potter and the Cursed Child* was announced. Set years after the titular Harry leaves Hogwarts, the play was to follow his children and their friends at Hogwarts. When it was revealed that a black actress, Noma Dumezweni, would be portraying the adult Hermione, a small but vocal group of fans had a negative reaction, likely because they had always pictured the character as white (possibly due to Emma Watson's movie portrayal), even though the canon never specifically identified Hermione's race. Rowling responded to the backlash with a tweet (above) to throw her support behind the casting choice.[1] Long before the play was cast, fans on Tumblr and other sites had been portraying Hermione as a young black girl in their art, stories, and other fan-created media. Leveraging their own creativity and experiences to bring representation of other races, genders, and sexualities is something that fans have been doing forever.

Think, for a moment, about the stereotypical Austen fan. What does this person look like? What gender? Age? Socioeconomic status? Most of us probably picture similar things. In fact, I would bet Colin Firth's wet shirt that the majority of people imagine a typical Austen fan as female, middle-aged or older, and middle class. She is likely also white. But I asked you to picture the stereotype. Does this bear out in real life?

Deborah Yaffe immersed herself in Austen fandom (and detailed her journey in *Among the Janeites*), and what she found is that in many cases, yes, the makeup of the Austen fandom follows this stereotypical mold. She cites a 2008 survey that found that Austen fans range in their career and life choices (air traffic controllers to Dominican friars), but that the vast majority of the fan base is female.[2] She notes that the survey did not ask for fans' racial identities, but that her experiences at meetings like the JASNA Annual General Meeting corroborated that the fan base has shown to be predominantly white. Yaffe also took an excursion through England on an Austen-themed trip, where she noted that most of her companions were indeed women, the exceptions being the husbands who trailed along after their Austen-obsessed wives, and all of them were white.[3] However, Yaffe's exploration of the Austen fandom was almost entirely into the ways fans engage *offline*—that is, at in-person meetings, trips, and the JASNA Annual General Meeting complete with Regency Ball.

In this case, it makes sense that many of the people she would meet would be older, more established adults who have the means to travel to celebrate a beloved author. It doesn't explain, however, why they are predominantly women.[4] It also does not account for why they are predominantly white. Perhaps we might say it is because Austen was white and her stories are about white people. But are they? Hollywood and its various all-white movie casts would have us believe so, but was that actually the case?

According to Olivia Murphy, author of *Jane Austen the Reader*, the notion that Austen's worlds were entirely white does not fit with the reality of the time in which they were written.[5] She explains that the habit of collecting statistics about race and other demographics that we are so familiar with today was not something that was done during the Regency period, and there certainly weren't cameras or smartphones around to document every moment of every day. This means that the records we do have of what people looked like—paintings and other arts—were a small fraction of those who would have been living in England at the time. Furthermore, it is likely that the many people of color who did live in Austen's England were among the service class, and therefore did not have the means or the time to sit for portraits.

We *do* have some idea of the makeup of Austen's England, however. There are historical documents that can provide some insight, and in this case we have evidence of black people in England, among various social classes: Dido Elizabeth Belle[6] and Francis Barber[7] are just two examples who were known at the time.

A recent film has challenged this "whites only" idea in historical dramas and could pave the way for more filmmakers to greenlight casts with diverse representation. *Lady Macbeth* (which has no direct tie to the Shakespearean character or play) is set in the Victorian period and features multiple characters played by black actors.[8] In fact, Steve Rose notes that "there are practically more characters of color in *Lady Macbeth* than there are in all the Austens, Dickenses, and Downtons put together."[9] He continues by pointing out that our assumptions about historical Britain as entirely white has more to do with the films being produced today and modern fantasies of countries uninhabited by immigrants and foreigners than with the reality of England at the times the stories are set.

This assumption that Austen's novels are populated only by white people likely does come from her representation in contemporary film. And while we can't say definitively that this lack of diverse actors in Austen film has exacerbated a lack of diversity in Austen fandom, it certainly has not contributed to notable change. Defending the casting of only white actors in Austen adaptations as an intent to maintain "historical accuracy" not only rejects the reality of Austen's England, but could also be subconsciously saying to people of color who might otherwise embrace Austen that this is a world that does not include them, and is therefore not for them.

Considering the evidence of people of color living in Regency England, historical accuracy in costume dramas would be better served by the inclusion of people of color than their exclusion. But fans are not waiting around for Hollywood to change its ways, and increased representation is making its way into Austen fanworks. Fan spaces are consistently used by marginalized groups to address their own cultural concerns within the dominant representation provided by their source texts.[10] The "underground status" of fans, according to Henry Jenkins, fosters this creativity: they do not need to be concerned about Hollywood's budgets and bottom lines or selling their product to any particular audience.[11] Likewise, Austen fans use their creative power in creating gifsets, fancasting,[12] making art, and writing fanfiction to disrupt the white, straight, cisgendered world that dominates professionally produced Austen media.

Austen's texts leave fans a lot of room for interpretation when it comes to the appearance of characters. Mr. Darcy is tall, Emma Woodhouse is handsome, Fanny Price is pretty. Austen was more concerned with describing her character's personalities, relationships, and socioeconomic status than with what they looked like. When she does offer physical descriptions, they have more to do with demeanor than with skin, hair, or eye color. We all remember Darcy's appreciation for Elizabeth's fine eyes or that Fanny Price is shy and awkward. But nowhere does it say that Captain Wentworth has dark hair or a jawline so sharp you could cut yourself on it. Of course, there is a point during Elizabeth's visit to Pemberley that Miss Bingley remarks at her being "very brown," which Darcy acknowledges would be expected of someone who is traveling in the summer. Given that we were not provided a description of how dark or light Elizabeth's skin tone was upon her first meeting the Bingleys, it is difficult to draw a clear comparison of her skin before her travels and after. There is also a point in *Mansfield Park* where Mary Crawford is introduced and described as having a "clear brown complexion," which is noted the Bertram sisters do not find competitive at all, even though she is pretty, because of their own paleness and attractiveness.[13] This reinforces the idea that pale skin was prized among the upper classes as a sign of leisure and a life free from labor, but this is no way implies that every Austen character imagined has be white. In fact, in the case of Mary Crawford, it is likely that she was darker skinned, since she and her brother are set up to be a contrast to typical aristocrats like the Bertrams.

The general lack of canonical physical descriptions for characters, and the increased visibility granted by the Tumblr, Pinterest, and other social media platforms that are harnessed by fans give creators a wide open sandbox in which to play around with how they might choose to represent their favorite Austen heroes and heroines. While we know this representation of nonwhites in Austen fandom exists, it can be difficult to find because it simply does not appear to be a large subset (yet). It is possible, though, through some diligent exploration, and the use of the right search terms, to locate fans who are pushing the boundaries of what people expect when they hear "Jane Austen." One great thing about fandom cultures online, too, is that finding one thing will often lead you to dozens more. For example, a search for Jane Austen and fancasts on Tumblr led me to some quick doodlings by user macaroon22, in which she features short snippets from *Pride and Prejudice*, drawn as people of color.[14] At the bottom she credits another user as her inspiration, and down the rabbit hole of Tumblr I went, digging for examples of fanart featuring non-white characters. The Tumblr user valeriemperez has several race-swapped fan pieces for different fandoms, one of which features English actress Gugu Mbatha-Raw as Mary Crawford from *Mansfield Park*. Interestingly, the images chosen to represent Mary are from Mbatha-Raw's portrayal of Dido Elizabeth Belle in the film *Belle*, who, we mentioned earlier, was a real-life mixed-race woman living in Regency England. The images, in keeping with the slightly wild and cheeky (at least compared to the Bertrams) characterization of Mary Crawford, show Mbatha-Raw styled in eighteenth-century gowns, running and laughing with a friend and offering wry smiles to others (who are not pictured).[15] Another user, lasocialista, created an entirely black fancast of *Pride*

Everybody is taken in at some period or other

Figure 4   Gugu Mbatha-Raw as Mary Crawford from *Mansfield Park*. Courtesy of Tatiana Hullender (Tumblr: valeriemperez).

and Prejudice[16] that also features Mbatha-Raw, along with Idris Elba, Angel Coulby, Ruth Negga, and Chiwetel Ejiofor, among others.

Race swapping is an exceptionally common practice among artists and other users on Tumblr. Some who can boast the skills of drawing and painting are able to create their own artwork and therefore draw the characters however they wish.[17] Another common way of race swapping characters is by creating gifsets or image sets, like those created by users valiriemperez and lasocialista. In this case, creators may spend hours looking for images and clips from other more representative movies, television, interviews, magazines, and so on, of their chosen actors or actresses, and then (often through their extreme powers of Photoshop and image editing) piece them together with text, titles, colors, and other images. Both of these efforts, creating and drawing original characters and editing together images and gifs, are incredibly time-consuming, labor-intensive work on the part of the creators, and show how devoted some fans are to Austen and to having inclusive representation in adaptations and variations of her work.

Because mainstream Hollywood production houses still tend to cast mainly white leads (though we acknowledge that this is changing and there have been efforts in recent years to increase diversity in casting), fan spaces like Tumblr are sometimes the only places for fans to turn to find the diversity or representation lacking in mainstream media. Consider, for example, another large online fandom: Harry Potter. Long before a black woman was cast as Hermione in the stage production of *The Cursed Child* and Rowling gave her enthusiastic support for the portrayal, artists were drawing Hermione as a young black girl.[18] Art and image sets depicting a black Hermione saw a resurgence on various social media platforms following the casting announcement for the play, bringing more visibility to the diversity that fandom can add to a person's individual experience of a text.

Imagined casting is not the only place where fans insert diversity into Austen's worlds, though. Naturally, the world of Jane Austen fanfiction also offers the opportunity for fans to explore the identities of Austen's characters. Rather than race swapping, which tends to happen more in visual expressions such as art, comics, or film, fanfiction is home to other kinds of representation, such as changing characters' genders or sexualities.[19] In addition to of-

Figure 5   Race-swapped illustration of a scene
from *Pride and Prejudice*. Courtesy of Jade Butler
(Tumblr: macaroon22).

fering greater representation that may be lacking in mainstream media, the
act of inserting a race, gender, or sexual identity into books such as Austen's
also serves as a way for fans to explore, develop, and experience *their own identities*. Sarah J. McCarthey and Elizabeth Birr Moje discuss this idea in "Identity
Matters," where they point out that both what people *read* and what people
write helps shape identity.[20] Specifically, people want to read about people
that they can closely identify with, and often, by engaging in writing, people
can come to understand themselves and their own identities.

On one level, understanding that people largely identify with novels and
other texts through their recognition of themselves in a character helps explain Austen's popularity among women, and the prolific amount of fan writing that is done within Austen's megaverse. Women, and given the current
slate of film adaptations, especially white women, can identify with Austen's characters and stories because she is writing about things that matter
to them, about people who are seen to be similar to them. (Who hasn't had
that Elizabeth Bennet experience of the creepy person who won't back off no
matter how uninterested you are? Though for most us, it is probably not our
cousin.) However, when you are a member of a marginalized group, such as
the queer community, it can be difficult to find mainstream media, and Austen adaptations specifically, where you might see yourself represented. So
what do you do? You turn to fandom, where you can look for others you iden-

tify with, and even explore your own identity by engaging in common fandom practices, like fanfiction, within a supportive, encouraging community. The overwhelming "whiteness" of much of Austen fandom may push people to creating fanworks to claim a place in Austen or to reconstruct the texts for different racial or gender identities.[21] This helps transform the experience of Austen from one of consuming a fictional world to a world of performance, and that performance can help lead them to a greater understanding of themselves and the community in which they live. They are also doing the service of carving out a space in the fandom for future fans who may be like them.

Elise Barker discusses the importance of identifying with characters specifically within Austen fandom when writing for *Persuasions On-Line*.[22] She discusses how fans "play" with Austen through various fan experiences, such as taking "Which Jane Austen Heroine Are You?" quizzes. She explores the idea that character identification is how readers understand a novel, and why, in some cases, that can be a problem: "One problem with character identification as the primary or exclusive means through which readers come to understand a novel is the fact that identity politics may make it difficult for some readers to commune or identify with a character who is different from the reader."[23] There are, of course, many fans who read certain Austen characters as queer with canonically supported evidence, such as Charlotte Lucas, Frank Churchill, and Emma Woodhouse.[24] Through the process of reading, fans look for cues and signs of how someone who identifies the way they do performs or creates identity, that is, "This is something a character like me does." Literature is a place where, in some cases, we learn *how to be*, and to go further, in writing we are *practicing being*, so fanfiction writers are both learning and practicing their own identities in relation to Austen's worlds and characters and finding spaces for themselves in places Austen may not have originally designed for them. This is part of the joy of being a fan: finding a place for yourself in a world you love, surrounded by characters with whom you identify. Additionally, Barker also explains that as much as one can construct identity by how we define ourselves and how we are *like* characters, we can also construct identity by defining ourselves as *different* from characters.[25] Both are ways fans can interact with a text and construct their own identities as a result. Fan spaces are unique places where fans can not only consume, but produce art and content for themselves and other fans, which can help give meaning to their lives and deepen their understanding of the texts and themselves.

It should come as no surprise that Austen fanfic writers play around with the worlds and characters in a variety of fun, interesting ways. When it comes to swapping genders, sexualities, or race, the variations are practically endless. In some cases, the changes are quite straightforward, as is the case with *Prejudice and Pride* found in the Archive of Our Own (AO3) miniature archive orphan_account.[26] In this reimagining, all the characters we know and love have been cisgender swapped (when assigned-at-birth binary genders are swapped in fiction to another binary gender), making the Bennet sisters all men, Darcy a woman, and so on.[27] In this way the writer explores how the characters' dynamics might have been different if the assigned biological genders were switched.[28] In other cases, such as a *Pride and Prejudice* alternate universe titled *Mr. Darcy's Vice* (originally published as a free fic on AO3 but now self-published as an ebook on Amazon), multiple types of swapping happens.[29] In this particular story, Darcy remains a man but is instead gay, and per certain expectations of men of his station at the time (such a marrying to produce an heir), attempting to suppress his sexuality. That is, until he meets Elias Bennet, heir to Longbourn in Netherfield. Here we can see that Elizabeth has been cisgender swapped, but most of the other characters remain as they were. These two stories both retain the original time period, so as one would expect, these changes significantly alter the dynamics of the characters and their situations in life. The Bennet daughters in *Mr. Darcy's Vice*, for example, would not be at risk of losing their home, as Elias, as a man, is able to inherit legally. In *Prejudice and Pride*, the stakes for the Darcy and Elizabeth characters are quite changed, as expectations of a woman of Mr. Darcy's stature would be quite different from his original situation, especially when one considers the stark difference between a women marrying down from her original class (and who would therefore decrease her social standing) and a man, who would retain his and increase his wife's by comparison.

The writers do not always deal with the intricacies of social norms and societal context, however. In *Prejudice and Pride* the author merely swaps the pronouns for each character, and the story left tends to lean more toward humor and satire than to serious consideration of the changing dynamics. It can be quite entertaining, though, to read of a Mr. Bennet exclaiming about Netherfield Hall being let at last, and Mrs. Bennet being dry and indifferent. Or to hear Lionel (the male version of Lydia) pestering Miss Bingley (as Mr. Bingley) for a ball or dreaming about officers. In a way, this fanfiction reimagining of the characters is satirizing Austen's social satire, making it both fun and entertaining to read but also (whether intentionally or not) poking at the framework within Austen herself that was working during her time. The author is doing to Austen's work what Austen herself was doing to the social world in which she lived.

These explorations that play with gender and sexuality offer, then, multiple layers of engagement with Austen's works. Readers can confront how ridiculous some of the social norms of the time appear when genders are changed, can laugh in a way that Austen's contemporaries might have at her skewering of the upper classes, and see the characters struggle with the same things they might, such as when Mr. Darcy, in *Mr. Darcy's Vice*, struggles with his identity as a gay man.[30] Rather than diminishing Austen, these fan creations can actually make them more complex, relatable, and interesting for a contemporary audience who does not want to let go of the characters they love so dearly. They also allow fans to heighten their experiences of the original texts by allowing them space to experiment with, and better understand, their emotional reactions to the original events or characters. When key elements of a story are changed, Constance Grady explains, it reminds readers of the source material, and all the emotional entanglement they have experienced upon first reading, thus enhances their engagement.[31]

Other Austen fic will take the characters, swap their identities in some way, and set the story in a more contemporary time, with updated plotlines and characters, so as to keep the original themes yet change the context. For example, the Elliots' distaste for Anne's romance with Captain Wentworth in *Persuasion* on the basis of his career and financial situation may not resonate as much with today's world because social classes have changed and are more fluid. But—swap a binary gender and sexual identity, such as in "A Very Wentworth Christmas," written by rosefox on AO3, and the original tension has a much more modern equivalent.[32] In this short piece, Frederick Wentworth and Andrew (Anne) Elliot are recently married and celebrating Christmas with

Wentworth's family. In one scene, Andrew admits to feeling more welcome in the Wentworth home because they are more open and accepting of the queer community than his own family. This is something modern-day readers, especially those who may identify as part of the queer community, can deeply understand: many face this kind of prejudice from their own families and friends, and seek out acceptance and family elsewhere. The same themes that Austen explores in *Persuasion* ring true in this fan reimagining: knowing yourself to be someone your family might never understand, finding love with someone your family disapproved of, and embracing a future of happiness with people who accept and love you, rather than clinging to family out of displaced loyalty.

Additionally, while race swapping is more often done in visual arts, some fanfic writers have chosen to use this technique when writing, as well. As is the case with *A Question of Seduction* by lizcommotion, the author chooses to tell the story of Anne de Bourgh, the daughter of Lady Catherine and a slave (though Anne was raised as a legitimate child of her adopted father).[33] The story follows Anne's relationship with Charlotte Lucas, who has married Mr. Collins as in the original text and resides at Rosings Parsonage while still clinging to her unrequited love for Elizabeth Bennet.[34] Following the death of Lady Catherine, Charlotte and Anne grow close, and begin a romantic relationship, with Anne's situation in life being complicated by both her mixed heritage and her sexuality.[35]

These changes to Austen's canon and insertion of different identities for her characters can keep the stories exciting and fresh, especially if we know that of course Anne (or Andrew) Elliot and Frederick Wentworth are going to end up together, but *how* they get to their happy ending is the fun part. If that journey is made more complicated by circumstances such as gender, race, or sexuality, then it adds an additional layer for the writer and reader to work through as we wait for the slow-burning romance to combust. At the same time, this also allows fans who may identify with these underrepresented communities to create and find spaces for themselves in Austen's world that may not explicitly have been drawn for them in the original text. Additionally, it allows fan writers and readers to examine the themes and ideas of Austen's texts through new lenses.

Outside of fan-created content, Janeites who want more diverse representation in their Austen adaptations, but perhaps do not want to create it themselves, can find it off the silver screen in places like Pemberley Digital's web
series of *Pride and Prejudice* (*The Lizzie Bennet Diaries*) and *Emma* (*Emma Approved*),
both available on YouTube. These two adaptations were set in a contemporary
world, and they took advantage of the changed setting to intentionally diver-
sify the casts, as would be fitting for a modern world. *The Lizzie Bennet Diaries*,
for example, features Fitz Williams (in place of Colonel Fitzwilliam) as a black,
gay man. The Bingleys become Bing Lee (Mr. Bingley) and Caroline Lee (Miss
Bingley), and are portrayed by Asian American actors. Finally, Charlotte Lucas
is instead Charlotte Lu, also played by an Asian American actor. The creators
also updated the storylines so that marriage is not the end goal for most of
the women characters (Mrs. Bennet being the exception, of course). Instead,
the women worry about finishing school, handling student debt, and finding rewarding careers that actually pay them a living wage. If there was ever
a modern equivalent for the uncertainty faced by the young Bennet sisters
and the threat their futures posed, *The Lizzie Bennet Diaries* tapped into those
fears of young, contemporary women across the world and made their stories
relatable for a modern audience. If they also happen to find love along the
way, great, but it isn't the primary motivation for a lot of the main characters.
(Charlotte, in fact, has no romantic storyline. Her entire plot is based around
her career development and growth.) Pemberley Digital was able to update a
beloved story for a modern audience, with a cast much more reflective of the
realities of today's world than if they had adhered to the (historically inaccurate) tradition of an all-white cast. Of course, most of the nonwhite characters were secondary or minor, so while the increased representation was a
welcome change, there is still room for improvement before fans of all races,
genders, and sexualities can see themselves within Austen's worlds.

The other Pemberley Digital series to offer fans more diversity was *Emma
Approved*, whose cast had a more ensemble feel to it and featured nonwhite
characters with larger roles. The title character, Emma Woodhouse, is portrayed by Joanna Sotomura, a Hawaiian-born mixed-race actress. Frank Churchill, Jane Fairfax, Maddie Bates, and Izzy Woodhouse are all portrayed by
nonwhite actors as well. For a series set in modern-day California, this more

accurately reflects the multiplicity of races you would encounter on a regular basis living in that area. However, one thing both Pemberley Digital series could have done better was to increase the visibility of LGBTQ+ characters. Between the two series, only one makes an appearance, Fitz in *The Lizzie Bennet Diaries*, and then he is only seen on camera in a few episodes. No named character in *Emma Approved* identifies on the LGBTQ+ spectrum. So while the increased racial diversity was an improvement, more steps could be taken in future adaptations to incorporate characters with different gender and sexual identities.

In the case of *The Lizzie Bennet Diaries*, many fans did what fans do best and looked for their own ways to insert this lack of representation into the worlds. A common relationship pairing among characters was Lydia Bennet and Gigi (Georgiana) Darcy. While the two never meet on camera in the series, and both have known histories of relationships with the same man (Wickham), fans couldn't help but see the two as potential romantic partners because of their similar experiences, potential chemistry, and ways they felt the two characters could balance each other. This is not a common pairing among the original novel characters in canon-based, fan-created works, so it is a "ship" specific to this one adaptation. It might speak to fans' inference that Pemberley Digital has created a more open, accepting world for characters who may identify as bi or gay, and they felt that enough material existed that it was possible, if these two characters met, that sparks might fly. It also reflects the impact that the actors and adaptation choices can have on fan reactions. The choices by the actors who portrayed the two characters, and the production company who updated the storylines, certainly impacted how viewers of the show "read" these characters, and clearly they saw enough there to make it plausible that these two women, both younger sisters, both living in the shadows of older siblings, both being manipulated by the same man, could connect romantically if given the chance.

In modern contexts within fan-created and Hollywood-produced Austen adaptations, it simply makes sense for the characters to be racially and sexually diverse, as different identities are much more visible and rising awareness about the importance of representation has begun to impact media. There is no compelling reason for characters in Austen's stories *not* to be diverse, whether they are set during the Regency period, in the 1990s, or in today's world.

Some fans, especially those who consider themselves Austen purists, might argue that there is no compelling reason *to* change Austen's characters' race (which, again, is not explicitly given for any of her characters), gender identities, or sexual identities. The characters and their stories are lovely as they are, so why should we change them? While we understand the resistance to change Austen's work—because, after all, we are Austen megafans ourselves—there are reasons that increased representation in character portrayal and within a fandom matters; specifically, it can bring increased enjoyment and vitality to such a long-standing fandom. Additionally, fans, illustrators, and movie producers have been deciding what Jane Austen and her characters look like for decades, as Devoney Looser details in *The Making of Jane Austen*. The choices made by who and what to illustrate in early printed versions of the novels, who to cast in the films (Laurence Olivier set a "type" for Darcy that has been maintained ever since), and what details to alter has always impacted what readers, fans, and scholars took away from Austen's novels.[36] Changing key details about characters or novels is not *new* to Austen's oeuvre; fans are just, like always, seemingly more willing to push boundaries than those who are producing something for profit may be. If an Austen adaptation can include zombies, then there is certainly room in twenty-first-century Janeism for people of color and LGBT+ representation.

Ask a fellow Jane Austen lover about their favorite novel, or their first time reading Austen, or why they keep rereading the same novel over and over again, and the answers may vary, but the emotion behind them will remain constant: Austen's novels matter to us, and are more than just books. The reasons may be different, but no matter which book you read first, there was something about these worlds, these characters, and these lives that brought you back, and keeps bringing you back. If you are involved at all in any part of Austen fandom—fanfiction, JASNA, collecting Austen-themed bath accessories or tote bags—it is clear that many Austen fans have a deep emotional attachment to the stories and the author. It may be that you identify with a specific character, or you read Austen first during an incredibly formative time in your life. Regardless, everyone has a gateway that leads them to their favorite authors, and something magnetic that will keep bringing them back. When that fandom is also looking at such a small collection of primary texts, the additional engagement that fandom offers can be a treasure: an opportunity to meet fans that love the same things you do, stories to read so you never have to leave this world behind, art to pin on your Pinterest board or your kitchen wall. When a fandom has a finite amount of primary source material, as is the case with Austen, the lifeblood of the fandom relies on people's continued creation of new material for themselves and other fans to consume. That's why wide representation within the broader Austen canon matters. It is well documented that people identify most with characters that look like or remind them of themselves.[37] If we want to keep sharing Austen's works with a broad, contemporary audience, then those who might not initially see themselves in a strict interpretation of Austen may never be drawn into the fandom and, therefore, may never contribute to an ever-growing, vital fan space that *needs* them.

Additionally, the lines between online fan spaces and practices and media producer are blurring in what Henry Jenkins calls convergence culture.[38] Spaces and practices that used to be the domain of fans—blogs, spoilers, fanfiction, art, and so forth—are being sanctioned by media producers alongside the primary content, inviting fans to officially practice their fandom, sometimes with official media content, as long as they adhere to the rules put in place by the producing company.[39] Producers are even using elements of transmedia to invite fans to participate in the ongoing narrative. Pemberley Digital has done this with most of the web series it produces, including three Jane Austen adaptations: *The Lizzie Bennet Diaries* (*Pride and Prejudice*), *Emma Approved* (*Emma*), and *Welcome to Sanditon* (*Sanditon*).[40] In these transmedia adaptations, fans are invited to send questions to the characters that could then be answered in a future episode, interact with the characters on Twitter, and in some cases even appear in the shows themselves.[41] The ubiquitous use of the internet by fans and producers alike has drawn these two previously separate spaces ever closer, making it easier for fans to interact with, and potentially influence, those in charge of the official storylines.

One way fans of media have influence on producers is by voicing support for shows through channels far outside Nielsen ratings and box office sales:

social media. In those long-ago days of before the internet, fans of canceled television shows, for example, might start letter writing campaigns and flood producers' offices with pleas to save their favorites. In some cases, they were successful in bringing back shows, if only for one additional season. Today it is much faster and easier to start a trending hashtag on Twitter, write an open letter, or send an email. And the power to reach and mobilize thousands (millions even) of other fans is unprecedented. Recently, when the fan-favorite and critical-darling television show *Brooklyn 99* was canceled by its home network, fans took to Twitter, Instagram, Snapchat, Facebook, and other platforms to express their outrage and plead for the show to continue. What happened? In less than two days it was picked up by another network.[42]

Whether or not show producers listen and respond to their fans' questions or suggestions on platforms like Twitter and Tumblr can vary depending on the show. In some cases, show writers will insert things into scripts as a direct response to fan feedback on social media.[43] This increased power of fans and activists can influence how films and television are made from the start, too. Recently, actor Ed Skrein, who is white and English, withdrew from playing the part of a character who is Japanese American in a film adaptation of a comic book after a large social media outcry over the whitewashing of the character.[44] It is not much a stretch to imagine that, should the Austen fandom become increasingly diverse and demanding of more representation in films, shows, and art, that creators may respond favorably. Indeed, such a move would not be without precedent, as the recent film *Before the Fall* is a reimagining of *Pride and Prejudice*, set in Virginia and featuring the traditional Darcy/Elizabeth romance instead as two men who fall in love despite their initial animosity toward each other. And, of course, there is the well-known Bollywood *Bride and Prejudice*, which incorporates Indian culture and Bollywood cinematic themes into Austen's timeless story and stars Indian actors in most of the main roles. If an American author can insert zombies into *Pride and Prejudice* and end up with a *New York Times* best seller and a movie adaptation, we are sure there is room in the Austen oeuvre for increased diversity of live humans. It may just have to be, as change often is, driven by the fans.

6

Pride, Prejudice, Zombies, and the Horror Mashup AU

HOLLY

I do not know which I admire more, Elizabeth Bennet. Your skill as a warrior or your resolve as a woman.

—Lady Catherine de Bourgh, *Pride and Prejudice and Zombies*

When Seth Grahame-Smith published a *Pride and Prejudice* horror parody novel in 2009 featuring Elizabeth Bennet slaying zombies in the middle of a country dance in Meryton, I was, I must admit, skeptical. Did I love Jane Austen's novels? Yes. Did I love a good zombie movie? Yes. Did I ever *think* that putting those two together would be a fantastic idea? Nope. Surprise—because somehow it worked. Critics at the time loved it. It climbed onto the *New York Times* bestseller list, and required a second printing in the UK.[1] Austen fans either raved about it or hated it with every fiber of their bonnet-wearing beings. Regardless of Janeites' personal feelings, a short five years later, in 2016, the film adaptation[2] rode the horror-parody genre[3] into theaters worldwide.

I feel I need to make a confession here before moving on, realizing that individual feelings about *Pride and Prejudice and Zombies* and its accompanying film can be a polarizing topic: I was lukewarm about the book, but I absolutely, unabashedley, *loved* the film. Perhaps the comedy and simple ridiculousness of the entire concept translated better in a movie than in the text, at least for me. Perhaps actor Matt Smith as a bumbling country clergymen *just worked*. Regardless, I felt the need to be transparent, knowing that many an Austen fan will vehemently disagree with me on the subject. I hope, if your feelings are quite the opposite, you can still join me on this exploration of the Austen/horror mashup and what it may mean for Austen's works in pop culture today.

One conversation that crops up around Austen again and again is her feminism. Indeed, we have kept returning to that concept repeatedly throughout this book. Is she a feminist? Are her novels feminist? Can she even be fairly judged as a feminist or not when that concept simply wasn't a thing during her time? The *Pride and Prejudice and Zombies* film (hereafter referred to as *PPZ*), brought on yet another wave of discussion around Jane Austen, Elizabeth Bennet, and feminism. It should be noted that Grahame-Smith was quoted in several interviews as saying that he did not add feminism into the mashup that wasn't already present in the original novel. He simply, in his words, took what Austen already did and "inject[ed] it with steroids."[4] This did not stop fans and critics from debating the film's feminism, however. Like *Pride and Prejudice*, both the adapted novel and film could reasonably be seen as both more or less feminist than their source material. One could even make the case that they are not feminist at all, showing that the debate around Austen's feminism is alive and well (unlike many residents of zombie-infested Meryton). Key differences exist between the novel and film versions of *Pride and Prejudice and Zombies*, and for the purpose of this text, we examine the film, directed by Burr Steers and starring Lily James as the zombie-slaying Elizabeth Bennet.

In this zombie-threatened world, women still inhabit the domestic sphere, while men are expected to be the defenders and protectors from the "unmentionables" (which is not a euphemism for underwear). Mrs. Bennet is still preoccupied with marrying off her daughters, and marriage is still the aim for respectable women. Charlotte Lucas says to Elizabeth during the ball at Meryton, "Zombies or no zombies, all women must think of marriage, Lizzie." Elizabeth, like her canon counterpart, still rejects the domestic role of dutiful, passive wife that society dictates to her, replying to Charlotte that the right man would never ask her to relinquish her sword for a ring (13:02).

Rather than making Elizabeth or the story more feminist, the film more accurately could be described as translating Austen's feminism so that it is more visible and recognizable to a modern audience. It is *differently* feminist. Casual fans of Austen today may not realize how radical Elizabeth Bennet and her actions and words were for a nineteenth-century woman. Among other actions, canon Elizabeth declined two eligible marriage proposals, spoke out of turn, refused to quiet her opinions in front of her social betters, and believed that her own feelings mattered in deciding the course of her life. These seem like normal, accepted freedoms to women today, but for Jane Austen and her time, a woman like Elizabeth Bennet was incredibly rare and revolutionary. As Claudia Johnson explains, "We tend to overlook or to underestimate Elizabeth's outrageous unconventionality," which, she explains, "constantly verges not merely on impertinence but on impropriety," especially when compared with fiction written by Austen's contemporaries and the conduct books in circulation at the time (seventy-five). Perhaps the best example of this translated feminism in *PPZ* occurs in the scene when Darcy proposes to Elizabeth the first time. Readers of Austen will well remember Elizabeth's rejection, where she assertively shames Darcy for his manners and disabuses him of all of his assumptions about her, her family, and her expectations of and feelings toward him. This rejection, and the forcefulness with which she expresses her opinions, make Elizabeth Bennet an uncommon, progressive heroine for her time. It does not always translate perfectly to a modern audience, however, who likely do not understand how radical it was for Elizabeth to refuse not one but *two* marriage proposals, especially one from a man of Mr. Darcy's station, and to speak so forcefully to a man, and one considered her social superior in many ways. Outspokenness in women was simply not the way in Austen's time. Elizabeth was rejecting multiple social expectations in her rejection of Mr. Darcy's proposal—both in the rejection itself, and in the manner of her rejection.

In *PPZ*, Elizabeth not only verbally declines Darcy's proposal but attacks him and initiates a room-destroying physical confrontation, with their sparring mimicking and reinforcing the verbal confrontation. Alexandra Sourakov, in her review for MIT's newspaper the *Tech*, points out that with the addition of this physical component, the film "highlights the force lurking in Jane Austen's original dialogues."[5] During Austen's time, as Sourakov notes, "words were the only weapons one could wield in polite society," and by putting a sword in Elizabeth's hands, and having her physically fight Darcy, it demonstrates the powerful blow her words struck in him. Wielding a sword itself does not make the film "more feminist," but it does translate what would have been obvious social commentary for the nineteenth century and makes Elizabeth's feminist attitudes and action more visible for women today, who may not fully grasp her unconventionality.

In addition to the sparring in the proposal scene, other details in the film's plot continue to reinforce the feminism of Austen's original text. Lady Catherine de Bourgh (sporting a fetching eye patch), for example, is renowned as the "best swordswoman" in Britain, and in the film's climax it is Elizabeth and Jane who brave the zombie-infested countryside to save their respective men. There are certainly characters who still believe that the men should slay the zombies and the women should keep the house, but the majority of the Bennets (Mrs. Bennet is the exception here), as well as Mr. Darcy, are not among them. Women taking up the fight against the unmentionables is not looked down upon, it is barely even commented upon in the film, except when judging social status by where the characters received their training (Japan for the rich, China for the wise). In fact, Miss Bingley chooses to try to put Elizabeth Bennet in her place by commenting on her Chinese battle training and not by bringing up her family's money or impropriety. A class system still exists, of course, but the markers by which women are measured have less to do with their birth and more with their (unconventional) education. This is likely much more relatable for a modern audience, who are used to sword-and-sorcery fantasy tales, zombie movies, and tropes such as training montages in comic books but are unaware of the social norms from the early 1800s. The film chooses to emphasize that it is not how we are born but what we choose to do with our lives that judges many a woman. By the end of the film, Lady Catherine, having tested Elizabeth against her toughest soldier, actually welcomes the Bennets into her home, going so far as to position Mrs. Bennet in a chair next to her own in one of the final scenes, almost marking her an equal, and does not object to a marriage between Darcy and Elizabeth.

One key plot point does not change, however, and that is that the heroine ends the story married to her hero. Marriage is still the primary goal for most women in this adaptation, as their economic long-term survival is still dependent on men, and the addition of zombies does not change that priority. However, the film departs from the novel in its conclusion: Grahame-Smith's novel ends with Elizabeth retiring her sword and giving up fighting when she marries; in the film, however, though she still marries Darcy, a final mid-credits scene depicts the two standing side by side, presented as equals, facing down an incoming zombie mob. Additionally, in Darcy's second proposal, rather than ask Elizabeth if she will be his wife, he asked her to "do [him] the great, great honor" of making him her husband. K. M. McFarland, in *Wired*, notes that the film does provide the women of the story more agency, and by bestowing the Bennet sisters (all of them) with zombie-slaying skills, they can "afford to seek a partner based on genuine affection."[6] McFarland's point, though, is only partially true. While their immediate survival (escaping the zombie plague) does not depend on a man, their long-term survival does, as they still live in 1813 and still cannot inherit property; the Bennet women still face being turned out of their house upon their father's death by their cousin, Parson Collins. This makes an advantageous marriage still important but not quite the most pressing, as death by brain eating is still the most immediate danger. But as the Bennet women prove on multiple occasions, they are well equipped to face that threat without a husband.

As mentioned earlier, fan reactions to *PPZ* were quite mixed. The film was considered a box office "bomb," as it did not make back the money spent to produce it. While critics were fairly harsh, fan reviews on sites like Rotten Tomatoes and Cinema Score leaned toward positive, with some Austen fans, like Jenna T, weighing in: "Wonderful film, I'm such a fan of Jane Austen and this movie did a wonderful combination of comedy and romance."[7] Another fan, Andy F, commented, "The cool thing about this movie is that it's the only version of Pride and Prejudice where that jerk Wickham doesn't get a happy ending." But not all fans were pleased with this particular Austen adaptation. Robin W commented, "Great, now it's ruined. This movie spat in the face of the 2005 classic. Very, very poor." Still other fans even refused to entertain the idea of a film adaptation of the novel parody, like Clinton P, who remarked, "Having read the wonderful book, I'm giving this film a miss. Do yourself a favor: re-read Jane Austen, then read the wonderful parody. I'm not willing to allow Hollywood to hijack my fun." It is clear from reviews and fan reactions that while there were plenty of reasons that many people enjoyed the film, just as many, if not more, were left confused. Viewers were sometimes unsure how they were supposed to respond. Was it intended to be funny? (Yes.) Or was it supposed to be scary? (It wasn't.) Was it a romcom? (Not by strict definition.) It certainly wasn't a sweeping drama. The combination of multiple genres into one piece, while it appeared to work for the book, is likely the primary reason the film did not achieve more success. Zombie fans wanted more gore and thrill, romance fans wanted more chemistry and interaction between Elizabeth and Darcy, and some Austen fans did not want any part of the movie at all. The film was certainly an experiment for Hollywood and Austen, and one that did not succeed when judged on the same scale as more traditional costume dramas or modern reinventions.

Fans that did enjoy the mashup, however, have continued to produce additional fanworks within this already adapted world. Archive of Our Own has a filter for *PPZ* (film) fanfictions, and images and gifsets can easily be found on Tumblr. Genre mashups are not incredibly common in Austen fanworks, but they do exist. Of all of Austen's novels, *Northanger Abbey* seems best situated for genre-bending, led as the story is by the fanciful Catherine Morland and her wild imagination. While the amount of fanfiction for *Northanger Abbey* in general is not terribly large (*Pride and Prejudice* definitely claims the top spot in Austen fanfic), it was pretty easy to find ones that played with horror and paranormal elements. One writer, HonoraryHobbit, posted a fic on fanfiction.net featuring a *Northanger Abbey/Dr. Who* crossover. In this short one-shot, the doctor and his companion land in the (literal) pages of the novel, meeting Catherine and Henry in the late Mrs. Tilney's room in the abbey. Other stories have inserted Catherine in Hogwarts[8] with Harry Potter and had her think that the Tilneys are vampires by blending elements of the *Twilight* novels with the original plot.[9] So while genre-bending within Austen is not an exceptionally common fan practice, it is not hard to find examples if one goes looking for them.

While searching for horror mashup fanworks online, I stumbled across another type of fanwork that blends horror with Austen. A fanfic writer created a *Northanger Abbey–Werewolves* Role-Playing Party Game mashup and shared it on fanfiction.net. In the traditional *Werewolves* game (which is similar in design to *Dungeons and Dragons*) players create characters, are given a setting, and "play" through a game created and directed by the narrator. The characters have to make decisions, overcome obstacles, and reach some kind of predetermined end goal.[10] In the Austen-centric version, players choose from a selection of Austen characters, and they play through the scenario provided by the writer. In this mashup, some characters are werewolves and others are villagers. It follows the conventions of online role-playing games, which use private chat rooms to interact with the other players online, allowing users from various geographic locations to play together, yet another way that the internet has revolutionized fandom.[11]

What does this new, zombie-slaying Elizabeth Bennet mean for Austen's place in pop culture? Is there a genre, art form, or medium that Austen *can't* be adapted to? If someone had asked me prior to the *Pride and Prejudice and Zombies* book publication if I thought there would ever be a Jane Austen horror film, I would have responded with a firm no. But it is obvious now that I would be wrong. Are her themes and stories so timeless? Fans keep coming back to them again and again regardless of form, genre, or time removed from the original publications. Scholars and fans write millions of words every year in Austen analysis or fanfiction. Elizabeth Bennet has been Mormon, Indian, a zombie slayer, and a modern-day professional woman working at a publishing house. And yet, through all of these, she is still recognizable as Austen's original creation: an independent, strong-willed woman who resists society's expectations of her and pursues her own destiny. She feels like a modern heroine to us, so it is no wonder that her story translates so well into so many contexts.

7 Why Don't They Just Kiss?
Sex and Identity in Austen

ZOE

Zoe: Diving speedoes cover ABSOLUTELY NOTHING

Holly: It's beautiful isn't it? 😝

Z: Literally when they do slowmo you can see their junk swing around

Like, why not just be nakey

H: BAHAHAHAHA. I haven't looked that closely! 😆

Z: There was just an INDECENT closeup

H: Perv.

Lol! Oh my god. I can't.

Z: I'm watching 3M finals at my desk while I clean up libguides

And they went in REAL close for a slowmo

H: Brb. Pulling up the livestream of Olympic diving.

—A text conversation between Zoe and Holly during the summer 2016 Olympics

When we think of Jane Austen we, as Janeites and scholars and modern readers, often think of the portrait now gracing the £10 bill. Jane, looking slightly homely, in a bonnet. She has kind, if tired, eyes, and she looks the picture of quiet and reserved womanhood.

But Jane is hiding a bounty of history behind that portrait. Jane's sexuality, or lack thereof, has been a part of scholarly speculation since the early Janeites. Austen's novels reek of propriety, but dig beneath the surface and there is a world of just-broken-off kisses, salacious dances, and barely buried sexual arousal.[1] Even some of the first Janeites were interested in the buried sexual or queer undertones to Austen's novels,[2] and the interest hasn't flagged with the creation and rise of the internet.[3] With the two hundredth anniversary of Jane Austen's death came the regular revisiting of the possible sexual relationship between Jane and Cassandra (Jane's sister), the "discovery" of sexual themes in her novels, and a general resurgence of interest in Austen's works.

We are going to explore how all of these "buried" sexual and identity themes show that queerness is, in a way, built into Austen. Austen herself may have been gay,[4] and novels so centered on the lives and loves of women were, and are, queer in many definitions, meaning both different and inclining toward the LGBTQ+. There is scholarship surrounding her queerest characters which ranges from observations of Charlotte Lucas's love for Elizabeth Bennet[5] to the possibility of Emma's lesbian leanings,[6] but these themes are also common in the fandom. One post on Tumblr by user penfairy begins with an ask-box submitted question reading "I didn't know there were Austen gay otps[7] (I'm very sheltered). Could you tell me what they are, please?" to which the Tumblr user penfairy replies (italics theirs), *"My time has come,"* before detailing two of the most common femslash[8] pairings: Lizzie Bennet/Charlotte Lucas and Emma Woodhouse/Harriet Smith.[9]

The fandom hasn't restricted itself to Tumblr posts and fanfiction reimaginings, either. The female-centric narratives and queer undertones have been reinforced throughout the history of performing Austen as well. Devoney Looser details the queer performances of Austen throughout history—the first performance as Mr. Darcy (Wellesley College, 1899) was by a woman as part of an all-female cast, and the actors leaned into the queerness of the performance, as "each actor approached her romantic part with gusto, including hand holding, shoulder grazing, and neck gazing."[10] Some may argue that since some of these all-women productions (which remained common through the early twentieth century) were not an uncommon practice; this is not a queer feature of the fandom or of adaptations. After all, Shakespeare was regularly performed by all-male casts. Yet it's impossible to ignore the queer readings of these performances, especially when one in particular—a stage adaptation of Eleanor Holmes Hinkley's *Dear Jane*—featured a lesbian couple (Eva Le Gallienne and Josephine Hutchinson) who had recently been outed by newspapers.[11] Queerness never leaves Jane far behind.

The modern fan response to Austen sits along the same lines as the all-female adaptations. There's a certain amount of "why not" and "why can't we" being asked in the fandom when questions of queerness are proposed. Why isn't Elizabeth Bennet bisexual? She seems deeply attached to Charlotte and can't seem to let her go to a (new) sexual, if not romantic, partner. Yet she does pine for Mr. Darcy, in the end. That strongly implies bisexuality. Why not have Emma be a lesbian? She rarely finds men worthy of her, and she admires Harriet and Jane so fiercely so as to be romantically attracted to them. That implies women loving women. What is the harm in seeing a reflection of yourself in the texts that we (including myself, as a queer fan) hold dear? Fandom has looked at that, across history, and has said, "There's no reason why not. Cast a lesbian partnership. Cast a female Darcy. Make it gayer. Make it queerer."

What is the point, however, in fans *wanting* two characters to be together when they know the end of the story is going to thwart their hopes? Why do we still hope that Emma and Harriet get together at the end of the novel even though we *know*, we have *read*, we have *memorized* the speech that Mr. Knightly gives to Emma as they declare their love? After all, these are finished novels. Austen isn't going to rise from the grave and write a coda to *Emma*. So why even hope? Charlotte Geater explains: "We never expect our [LGBTQ+] ships to become canon. That's the first thing you need to know . . . we never expect our favourite relationships — the potentially romantic relationships we see between characters in the stories the world tells us — to be sanctioned by anyone but us."[12] Fans ship[13] characters in queer relationships not because the queerness is going to happen, but because the loop never closes: there is always unsurety in romance and in sex and in identity, and to use queer subtext to ship characters or to cast characters or to imagine characters is to use that open loop.

The shipping, the act itself, uses the complexity found outside of straight-forward storytelling (pun intended) and injects "how people struggle to allow themselves what they want."[14] We know that Elizabeth and Darcy end up together, that Emma and Mr. Knightly will realize their love, that Charlotte will marry Mr. Collins, but they don't have to. They can do something different. "Shipping puts relationships back at the centre of the story. Choices. Desires. It's not a joyless part of the formula of a . . . narrative any longer."[15] There don't have to be man-meets-woman-therefore-man-and-woman-fall-in-love plots around every corner. The characters are, in a way, real people, with their own desires as complex as our own. Maybe this time . . . things are different. This time the queer ship we wish for is going to happen. Even if we have to write it ourselves.

I should rephrase; sometimes we, as queer fans, do get our wish, but sometimes you have to be careful what you wish for. Representation doesn't always mean a *good* or *flattering* or even *accurate* representation. The LGBTQ+ community has dealt with queerbaiting,[16] Bury Your Gays,[17] and underrepresentation so much that sometimes representation feels like a gift even when it is poorly done. Unfortunately, a recent (2016) modern novel adaptation of *Pride and Prejudice* called *Eligible* (Curtis Sittenfeld) offers an example of exactly this issue.

Eligible was written as a part of the Austen Project, a project to rewrite and adapt the six finished Austen novels as modern stories, and was the adaptation of *Pride and Prejudice*. The books in the Austen Project received mixed reviews[18] and *Eligible* is easily both the most well-known as well as the highest rated of the adaptations.[19] The story itself provides a fun and lighthearted, for the most part, rewrite of *Pride and Prejudice*. Everyone is aged up so as to provide a more realistic foundation for a modern fear of not being married, sex is treated as a part of the dating or hookup process, and Kitty and Lydia are transformed into hot-yoga- and crossfit-loving trend followers. But the veneer of fun covers serious representation issues in the novel that both pull from some commonly held subtext and twist them. The trouble begins with Mary Bennet. It's hard to like Mary Bennet, canon version or otherwise. She's boring, her family doesn't really respect her or her desires, she clearly wants to be the best and most proper, but as Terry Pratchett once wrote, she mistakes mannerisms for manners.[20] In *Eligible* her character becomes a punchline more often than not, and the family's jokes revolve not around her insistence on specific readings from boring theological texts or her desire to be the most proper—to a fault—but instead they focus on the family's jokes that Mary is probably a lesbian.

(That Mary is a lesbian is a commonly held fan theory, it should be stated.[21] Sittenfeld did not come up with this subtext on her own. And it's also true that Mary is, very often, the butt of the joke in *Pride in Prejudice*, whether it's her distaste for balls, her awful singing, or her moral philosophizing, but her sexuality is not a joke; it is subtext read by a modern audience that fits the subtext that we recognize as implying a coded lesbianism. Whether Austen wanted that subtext to be read as such is impossible to know unless you've got a particularly reliable medium on call, and the fact of lesbians and LGBTQ+ folks aside, women loving women sexually was not considered a viable option in the era. All of that said, this "representation," well, isn't.)

When Mary disappears on weeknights to a private activity the joke is that she's doing something gay. And, as the *LA Times Review of Books*'s blog points out, when it's revealed that her activity is merely bowling, the family is deeply relieved, as though having someone queer in the family would be the downfall of their place in society.[22] It's not necessarily unthinkable that the Bennet family, so held with traditional morals—or so they would like you to believe—would be uncomfortable with having a lesbian in the family. It happens across the world every day that LGBTQ+ folks come out to their family to a poor reception. If that had been the case, Sittenfeld could have dealt with that issue, or simply pointed out that the Bennet family are, in fact, sort of terrible. Instead, *Eligible* invites the audience to laugh at Mary *with* the Bennet family and to join in on their relief when she turns out to be bowling instead of being gay. Unfortunately, the issues of representation don't end with Mary.

Wickham is, traditionally, like Willoughby before him, a rake—a rogue. He's a breaker of hearts, emotionally manipulative, and possibly a pedophile. He's not a good guy. Canonically, the *reason* that the Bennets are so ashamed of Lydia stems from these characteristics; Wickham is mired in debt, he is living in sin with their daughter, and he is clearly after what little money they have, should he be convinced into marrying Lydia at all. He can be a tricky character to modernize without making him cartoonish, and the situation in general can be difficult to translate into our way of thinking of sex and marriage today; after all, premarital sex is hardly considered taboo in much of the literature and media consumed by modern audiences, and beloved antiheroes abound in storytelling. In an earlier chapter we discuss the excellent (if difficult to watch) adaptation of Wickham in *The Lizzie Bennet Diaries*, but *Eligible* does a less stellar job.

In the case of *Eligible*, the choice was made to split Wickham into two parts. There's the traditionally cardboard not-a-good-guy that Lizzie is having an affair with (an extension of her canonical closeness and flirtation), who has

Wickham-like sensibilities and is, clearly, not a great human being. That is Jasper Wick. The other part of Wickham is split into a crossfit gym owner, named Hamilton Ryan, who runs off with Lydia. This is where the issues of homophobia and transphobia come to a head. In many reviews of *Eligible* this relationship is barely mentioned, and in a few it's brushed aside as simply being a quirk of the Bennet family, rather than a piece of media holding up the structures and stereotypes that allow transphobia to continue. You see, Hamilton Ryan is a transman. The *LA Times Review of Books*'s blog wrote this about the plot reveal:

> As one sister reveals to another via a frantic, sensational text: "Lydia and Ham eloped to Chicago. Turns out Ham transgender/born female!!!! M & D freaking out." Mr. and Mrs. Bennet find the romance "strange and disgusting" and suggest that Ham has missed his chance to be "one of Barnum's bearded ladies." "Mrs. Bennett" [sic] promptly decides to cut Lydia out of the family, lamenting the grandchildren she will never have and the "waste" of Lydia's beauty.[23]

Again, this reveal could have sparked an interesting conversation within the novel or a conversation with the reader by acknowledging the, frankly, horribly transphobic reaction of the Bennet family. Instead Liz asks about Hamilton's genitals, and Darcy—the hero of the novel and a doctor, to boot, in this adaptation—helps the Bennet family theoretically find peace with their daughter's decision by labeling Hamilton's gender as a "birth defect" rather than providing this family with genuine information on dysphoria, transphobia, and gender spectrum. This could have been a good place for the author to invite the readers to acknowledge that the characters in the novel are far from good people, but instead the *Avidly* blog put it best: "I couldn't help but feel that the novel's desire to titillate a mainstream readership overpowers the liberal impulse behind Sittenfeld's inclusion of a wider range of sexual possibilities."[24] Sittenfeld does not provide actual representation here; the novel does not give an LGBTQ+ reader someone to identify with. The joke isn't laughing with the queer community, it's laughing *at* the queer community. It's homophobia disguised as "proximate diversity"[25] and representation. Sittenfeld has created a modern version of Mrs. Bennet's circus analogy:

an LGBTQ+ character on display for the straight audience to point at and say, "Look! Representation!"

Sittenfeld makes a half-hearted attempt to show that Liz is more accepting than the rest of her family, but the attempts are fumbling and far from showing Liz to be the open-minded woman she claims she is. Sittenfeld describes Liz researching "*kathoey* in South East Asia and the *salzikrum* of the Ancient Middle East,"[26] but she does not give any indication if she herself had done this research; there is no further mention of these terms or if they had religious, social, or even political, rather than gendered, meanings. She writes that Liz, who considers herself so enlightened as to know one other transgender person, actually asked her sister Mary if Ham had a fake penis. It wasn't until *after* that exchange that she managed, somehow, to learn that "it was, apparently, no less rude to ask about the genitals of a transgender person than about those who were nontransgender, or cisgender."[27] Amazingly, she manages to figure out that transgender people are people, too, and that asking about their genitals *might* be considered rude.

The good news is that Austen fans have everything from headcanon to fanfiction for fixing the representation problem. Because Austen is full of queer subtext, there's no need to shoehorn in homophobic or transphobic or LGBTQ+phobic plotlines to check the box marked "modern." As discussed earlier, these ships don't have to be possible; they represent the possibility of character interactions. The combination of shipping and fanfiction creates "the global realization that we need not wait for the right stories to fall into our laps; creative participation is the antidote to consumer dissatisfaction, not patience."[28] In many cases these pieces of creative participation are published online in communities such as fanfiction.net or Archive of Our Own, but in other cases they are published commercially. Some even make it to the screen.

One of the more intriguing suppositions made in fan-created content is that Caroline Bingley is herself queer. *Lost in Austen*, a four-part miniseries that aired in 2009, featured a self-insert fanfiction[29] for the small screen. While this was a mainstream movie, not an amateur fan production, we are going to consider it within the scheme of fan-made works, as the author of the screenplay employs techniques incredibly common in fanfiction. Fans on multiple blogs,[30] and scholars[31] in "traditional" publications[32] alike have pointed out the similarities in structure between this "professional" publication and more "amateur" works. And so we dive in as Amanda, the heroine of *Lost in Austen*, finds a portal in her bathroom that leads her straight into the world of *Pride and Prejudice*.

Amanda and Elizabeth Bennet swap places, but everything Amanda tries to do to preserve the narrative integrity of the original Austen story causes more problems. Misunderstandings and lies to rival a Shakespeare comedy lead to everyone marrying or falling in love with the wrong person, but in the end Amanda and Elizabeth agree to swap places permanently, and Amanda marries Mr. Darcy and lives (we assume) a happy life. Within the story, however, is a fascinating subplot. When trying to spurn the advances of Mr. Bingley, Amanda states that she is a lesbian and the word gets around to Caroline Bingley, who has been slowly teasing and sniping at Amanda the entire time. As Amanda packs to leave Pemberley, Caroline approaches her and announces that she, too, is a lesbian and has been watching Amanda closely. She wants to marry Mr. Darcy only to fulfil society's (and God's, according to Caroline) expectations for her and her place in society, but she says that she would never enjoy the company of a man. Amanda, who is not actually gay, spurns Caroline's advances.

This inclusion of Caroline Bingley as a lesbian is fascinating—it's true that in the canon novel she cares more for what society expects from her, and she is often found stating what men *should* want from a wife rather than what, from the actual displays of affection she might see, men *do* want from a loving relationship. This is, of course, expected in a society where love and marriage don't need to go hand-in-hand, but it could be read as a woman who has no interest in men trying to figure out how best to show that *they* should be interested in *her*. The portrayal is neither positive nor negative in terms of representation; Caroline does end up becoming the Suddenly Sexuality[33] trope and Amanda the Sorry, I'm Gay[34] trope, but within the long list of damaging LGBTQ+ depictions in modern media, these are small criticisms. The adaptation has simply taken a possibility presented in the subtext and made it text. By the end of the story Caroline is in the same position as she is in the canon novel, but the audience knows that she will continue to perform heterosexuality in order to fit into the period and society.

Interestingly, the pairing of Caroline and Amanda has gained some traction in the fandom. A search of YouTube brings up a shipping fanvid[35] for Caroline and Amanda. Representation and shipping can be found with any pairing!

The underlying queer themes encompass more than a single queer woman and a self-insert character, though. For those not in the know about the popular queer ships in Austen fandom, *Emma* features often, as does Lizzie Bennet and Charlotte Lucas's friendship. Tumblr user penfairy outlines the basic reasons, using actual canon textual evidence, that modern readers can draw an easy conclusion to gay (women loving women) ships in Austen. She focuses first on Emma Woodhouse and Harriet Smith. Although not as popular in modern fanfiction, this pair can be explicitly drawn from the canon and comes up often in academic works about queer Austen.

> Miss Smith was a girl of seventeen, whom Emma knew very well by sight and had long felt an interest in, on account of her beauty.
>
> (*Emma's been scoping out the new hottie in the neighbourhood from day 1.*)
>
> She was a very pretty girl, and her beauty happened to be of a sort which Emma particularly admired. She was short, plump, and fair, with a fine bloom, blue eyes, light hair, regular features, and a look of great sweetness; and before the end of the evening, Emma was as much pleased with her manners as her person, and quite determined to continue the acquaintance.
>
> (*Harriet, you beautiful tropical fish.*)
>
> She was so busy in admiring those soft blue eyes, in talking and listening, and forming all these schemes in the in-betweens, that the evening flew away at a very unusual rate.
>
> (*Time flies when you're fucking gay, am I right?*)[36]

Tumblr user penfairy isn't the only one to spot the implications of queerness in *Emma*, even without explicit fanfiction. Devoney Looser talks on *The Bennet*

Edit Podcast (as well as in the *Atlantic*) about how depictions of Emma as a lesbian date back to the 1950s.[37] During the bicentennial celebration of Austen in the summer of 2017, *BOOK RIOT* published a number of articles on the canon and their adaptations, and one focused on the queerness in *Emma*. Not in adaptations of *Emma*, but in the discovery of queerness in the text itself. Michelle Hart writes, "Reading Jane Austen when not-straight is kind of frustrating: the women are mostly great, witty and astute, and their inevitably male objects of affection are, well, not. (Yes, even Mr. Darcy). Women who don't buy into or care about the nonsense of men are Austen's bread and butter, her lasting legacy—or at least, a very large part of it."[38] Emma as a character encapsulates this feeling; she constantly moves against society's expectations for her, she flaunts her singleness and states that she will never marry, she surrounds herself with intimate female friendships and does not even seek the company of men. For Hart, it was clear—Emma is queer, if not explicitly gay. And for Hart, it was the first time she could see herself in Austen's material: "As I was reminded during Pride month last month, our queerness, our deviation from what is considered 'conventional' and our degree of freedom from gender norms, is something to be celebrated. As a young queer girl, reading *Emma* was a revelation."[39] Relatability is vitally important for readers to engage with a story, and finding clues between the lines, hints, or outright statements of queerness can mean a new understanding and appreciation of Austen's canon. The fact that the representation was in the original text rather than a fanwork only emphasizes how closely queerness is associated with Austen.

One of the most-fun queer Austen rewrites is less of a full story and more a selection of vignettes. The website Autostraddle[40] put together an article in 2016 titled "Every Jane Austen Novel If It Were Gay and Also Historically Inaccurate." The article provides cover graphics reimagining the cover art for these fictional books as though the rewrites were done in a pulp romance style, complete with cone bras but with one major change: all the covers feature two women rather than one man and one woman. Some of the summaries for these not-real-but-I'd-read-them books follow the plot of the original canon story only enough to be called an adaptation in the loosest terms. Others, though, dive headfirst into the plot and, well, make it gay. The *Sense and Sensibility* "adaptation," for instance, reads as follows:

Unmarried sisters Marianne and Elinor take to the countryside, having lost the favor of their wealthier brother and his sister-in-law. There, Marianne meets Brandalynn, a country gentlewoman who enjoys cigars and complicated cocktails, but spurns her because she thinks Brandalynn's too old for her and that her successful career as a large animal vet is unbecoming. Instead, Marianne is drawn to Wenda, a dashing and urbane young woman with the most fashionable of undercuts, who she meets while on a walk and who woos her with smoldering harpsichord ballads that she writes herself in the style of Chris Pureka. In the meantime, Elinor is getting closer to the enigmatic Edwina, who she's super into until she finds out that she's still living with her ex, Lucy Steele, who she doesn't have feelings for anymore but they share a dog and their apartment is rent-controlled and if Edwina moved out Lucy would probably have to move back in with her mom, and Lucy's mom is a total bitch. Marianne's heart is broken when Wenda ghosts[41] and moves to Portland to become a craft brewer, but decides to give Brandalynn another shot when she sees her on Tinder and finds that actually they really click. Edwina is suddenly single when Lucy moves out because she's met an up-and-coming fashionplate model, and she and Elinor are finally able to make it work.[42]

This summary-style adaptation hits every plot point of the canon novel in the space of a long paragraph and not only queers the story but modernizes it as well. The modern audience can read this summary and say, "Hey, I've swiped right on someone on Tinder because I've met them before, I wonder if this time it'll work," or "I know someone who got stuck living with their ex in an apartment because of the lease structure and I wouldn't touch that situation with a ten-foot pole," or even "Yeah, I've been ghosted before." These short adaptations don't fall into either the bury-your-gays or the single-and-solitary-token-gay trope. In fact, background characters are queered as well. In the *Pride and Prejudice* summary, Rachel, to describe the modernization of the Lydia storyline, writes, "When Elizabeth's younger sister Lydia gets a really ill-advised courthouse wedding with her annoying on-again-off-again girlfriend without consulting anyone first in the heady rush of the recent same-sex marriage legalization."[43] There's no need to change Wickham into a horrible woman: the point isn't that he's bad—or she's bad, if we're changing pronouns/cis-biological sex— it's that the Bennets are frustrated and scared for their daughter and that the Darcy character (Fiona, in this version) can step in and help. In this case, with a legal degree to figure out how to get a quick divorce. I have *met* these stereotypes in the LGBTQ+ community. Yes, I want to read this novel.

Part of the fun of these queer adaptations is their strong relatability. They're not just filled with LGBTQ+, they're also fun and relaxed in a way that many adaptations aren't when it comes to Austen. Austen's novels are *filled* with humor (I recommend *Lady Susan* if you don't believe me), but just as with Shakespeare, modern audiences sometimes take things only as they're written today, with today's context. Shakespeare is filled with "dick jokes" and "yo mama" jokes just as Austen is filled with wry observations about society and laugh-out-loud comments about etiquette and mannerisms, yet modern audiences don't have the cultural context clues to parse the jokes. Just like memes, queer modern adaptations make the novels accessible, and these adaptations in particular make them accessible to the queer community as well as the community at large. After being left off the invitation to classical literature for so long, these adaptations, the fanfiction, the theories, and reading between the lines are just another way to connect with stories that may have never resonated, or stories that audiences were always told were straight as an arrow and, well, maybe that arrow is a little crooked.

The crooked arrow in literature extends past the adaptations and into fanfiction. Autostraddle contributor Heather Hogan published an article in 2015 called "10 Lesbian Sex Scenes I Wrote Before I Had Lesbian Sex,"[44] which details the fanfiction she wrote featuring queer sex scenes between various characters. Austen features prominently: three of the ten excerpted fanfiction scenes are characters from Austen. Heather makes it clear to the reader that she understands just how terrible the writing in these scenes is, but that these scenes, and these characters, influenced her interest in women and her interest in women loving women. In fact, Heather describes the process of finding other women who love women writing about women who love women as heaven. For her, and for fans across the globe, seeing queer characters on the page, whether it's an internet page or a printed one, is a powerful experience.

The excerpts range in original content from *Star Trek* to *Princess Diaries* to *Austen*. In one of the Austen excerpts Elizabeth is a bisexual woman in love with both Mr. Darcy and with Charlotte, but it's with Charlotte she has sex in "the middle of the room where the Bennets kept their small art collection."[45] In the second excerpt (from a different story), Elizabeth furiously masturbates at the thought of Charlotte, and wonders how best to steal her away from Mr. Collins. In the final Austen lesbian story piece, Heather notes before presenting the excerpt that "I stand by my assertion that Jane Fairfax is the most prolific lover of all Austen heroines." The excerpt?

> Emma had been a fool and she understood this now. All the time she spent trying to set up Jane with the men in this neighborhood, it had just been a way for her to figure out what Jane liked so Emma could become that person. When Emma told Jane this, Jane cupped Emma's face in her hands and said, "Just be the person you are, my dear Emma. That's who I fell in love with."
>
> She slipped her tongue into Emma's mouth and her thigh between Emma's legs, and her orgasm was immediate thunder. She's never had anyone love her for exactly who she was before! Perhaps orgasms could be emotional too? Indeed she had just proven it![46]

This story section might be extremely poorly written (okay, yes, it is; they all are, and again, Heather acknowledges this) but it, and all the other excerpts are also indicative of the desire fans—and people in general—have to see characters reflecting themselves. Heather has taken Captain Janeway of *Star Trek: Voyager* and Emma Woodhouse of Austen canon and said, Hey, they're like me! They're lesbians! And here: have some scenes that prove it.

A lot of what I've covered here is specifically about the LGBTQ+ community. Historically, of course, lesbians "didn't exist" due to laws that prevented their relationships from being acknowledged or even legal.[47] We, as the LGBTQ+ audience—or as the modern audience, scholar, historian, and fan alike— seek representation in what we read and study, but beyond representation there still exists an interest in the sex in Austen's works. The 1999 *Mansfield Park* adaptation from the BBC begins with a graphic sex scene. Marianne and Willoughby may well have had sex. Certainly it's strongly implied that Lydia and Wickham do. In works that bleed sexual tension and witty banter, fans, scholars, historians . . . we want to see what happens *next* and behind closed doors.

Sex is buried in Austen all over the place and can be found in adaptations as well as the canon text. While Elizabeth and Mr. Darcy dance around each other at Pemberley, Lydia runs away with George Wickham, and in the most commonly referenced adaptation, the 1995 BBC *Pride and Prejudice*, Lydia and Wickham aren't just pictured together in London, they're pictured together, with underclothes hanging in the background, in a *bedroom* in London.[48] In the 2005 version starring Keira Knightley, Elizabeth and Mr. Darcy just barely prevent themselves from kissing one another after Mr. Darcy's first proposal—a scene, in this adaptation, shot in the pouring rain to emphasize the actors' bodies with damp clothing clinging just so.[49] In *The Lizzie Bennet Diaries* a kiss between Lizzie and Darcy becomes hot enough that they have to cut the camera. In fact, Elizabeth and Darcy get very, *very* busy quite often in many adaptations and modernizations of *Pride and Prejudice*. Sex-insert fanfiction[50] pops up in both the amateur and "professional" fanfiction world quite often and ranges from situations like *Eligible*, in which Liz and Darcy have sex but Jane is also trying to get pregnant via IVF, to *Mr. Darcy Takes a Wife*, a period piece that explicitly details the sex lives of Lizzie and Darcy while exploring the life after their marriage. These sex-insert fics theoretically swap the sexy background characters and situations (the Crawfords, for instance, or Wickham/Willoughby's pasts) for sexy, intriguing foreground situations; this time around, Lizzie and Darcy let their hate at first sight turn into hate sex at first sight and Wickham is all but forgotten.

These sex-insert stories toe an interesting line as relating to the canon material. Lydia and Wickham's relationship and marriage is scandalous both because of Wickham's debts and his rakish attitudes and because they are, as implied by the text, living in sin, in an apartment together in London. The 1995 BBC adaptation actually shows Lydia and Wickham together, complete with Lydia's underclothes tossed over a changing screen,[51] which only highlights the probable sex they were having. Canon or not, the scene reflects the worry of the Bennet family and the assumptions others would have made about Lydia. Given that, period-set sex-insert stories that give Elizabeth and Darcy an outlet for their sexual tension ride a difficult line. If they attempt to be close to period ideas in other ways, how would Elizabeth view herself, or her sister, given that she, too, has engaged in sinful activities? If there is no need to stray too close to canon or period-typical attitudes, there still remains the reputation question. Does Lydia exist in the story? How is her flirting viewed given the new (sexy) light?

Some stories simply do away with the conventions surrounding premarital or extramarital sex. Stories that describe queer sex, as discussed above, for instance, don't need characters to adhere to the period-typical views, since the characters are already eschewing the values of the time by engaging in what would have been considered illegal or sinful activities. Stories that focus on straight sex might flip convention and simply have all the characters engaging in lascivious activities, as is common in some of the most popular "explicit" fanfiction stories about the Austen characters on Archive of Our Own. The story "Pride and Prejudice Erotica," by user currerbell,[52] gives this summary: "Pride and Prejudice with steamy twist. The whole of England is in a sexual revolution and the characters of Jane Austen's most beloved book are experiencing it."[53] These stories simply throw caution to the wind and envelop all the characters involved in steamy sex. And like almost every Austen adaptation, article about Austen, or sufficiently well-read relative talking about Austen, this fanfiction begins with a version of, "It is a truth universally acknowledged," in this case continuing with "that a single man in possession of a good fortune, must be in want of a wife. In fact, what single men actually seek is an exceedingly good lay."[54]

These sexy fanfiction stories stem from Austen's incredible gift for writing characters who pine for and match wits against others. Kate Beaton, an incredible comic who specializes in historical and literary fun and jokes, and who has created more than one Austen comic, writes, "Are any of us really surprised that there is so much Darcy/Elizabeth fan fiction out there? Fan fiction was created for this. Aching stares from across the room can only go so far, if you know what I'm sayin'."[55] The comic above this comment shows Darcy holding Elizabeth by the shoulders and exclaiming, "Elizabeth I have come to ravish you," followed by a panel where Elizabeth holds Darcy close, his arms around her waist and hers around his neck, with ballgoers in the foreground. She whispers "Not in the middle of the ball, Mister Darcy," to which he exclaims "FINE," and in the third panel is pictured alone, in a chair, fists balled on his thighs, saying, "Then I will sit here consumed with lust for the rest of the evening."[56] Given the 1995 and 2005 film adaptations, which picture Darcy "firthing,"[57] and the canon text, where Darcy can't seem to keep his eyes off Elizabeth, this is an easy leap.

Yet Austen didn't write romance in our modern sense; she wrote social commentary for her time. Kate Beaton's first Austen comic[58] depicts Jane at her writing desk. A friend comes in and stands behind her and asks, "Are you writing another story with Mister Darcy?" to which Jane responds, "NO! This is a social commentary!" Her friend doesn't seem to care, resulting in this back and forth: "Is it a social commentary about hunky dreamboats?" "NO." "Is there a make out scene?" "LEAVE ME ALONE."

Why are we inserting sex? Yes, Darcy and Elizabeth clearly have chemistry, but part of their chemistry is based on the social norms that they both dance around and sometimes don't. Elizabeth isn't educated and wealthy enough to be considered in the same social sphere as Darcy. He writes her an impassioned letter after she *turns his offer of marriage down*. As an exceedingly wealthy man this would have been deeply unusual for him and in society. He goes out of his way to help a middle-class family to whom he no longer has a connection because of his love for Elizabeth. Yes, it's a romance because they fall in love and marry, but the *story* is about the social norms and commentary that exist in that society. Yet without studying Austen closely, modern audiences don't see those issues. What do they see? A classic modern romance. *Pride and Prejudice*: Guy meets girl. They hate each other at first glance. But they're both reasonably handsome and match wits. They grow to understand one another, then appreciate each other. They fall in love. *Sense and Sensibility*: Man and woman were once in love but couldn't do anything about it and also didn't tell each other. Man becomes engaged to someone else. They meet again. Both are still in love and the other engagement is broken off. They marry. Without the contemporary context these are chick-lit romances. So why not spice them up? And if we're going to spice them up, let's spice them up a *lot*. Because we love the romance of the characters and have lost the context for the social commentary.

Juliette Wells discusses the insertion of sex in Austen fanfiction and points out that it's not until recently that this type of fanfiction came about. She quotes Roger Sales talking about the juxtaposition of the buttoned-up Austen and the very unbuttoned sex as a major draw.[59] She discusses Linda Berdoll, author of *Mr. Darcy Takes a Wife*, who wrote in the preface, "What throbs fast and full, what blood rushes through, is denied her unforgettable characters and, therefore us. Dash it all! We endeavour to right this wrong by completing at least one of her stories, beginning whence hers leaves off. Our lovers have wed. But the throbbing that we first encounter is not the cry of a passionate heart. Another part of her anatomy is grieving Elizabeth Bennet Darcy."[60] *Mr. Darcy Takes a Wife* is a fantastic example of Austen sex-insert fanfiction. The author admits to being an avowed fan who just wanted to see what happened next, through our modern understanding of sex.

Sometimes vanilla, canon, heterosexual pairings aren't enough for what authors want. Ann Herendeen's *Pride/Prejudice* takes the Lizzie/Charlotte ship and expands on it, creating an adaptation where both Elizabeth and Darcy are bisexual and engaged in a same-sex relationship with others. The book dives into the characters' mindsets, creating not just a sexy romp, as depicted in *Mr. Darcy Takes a Wife*, but a fleshed-out story (pun intended). The book opens with an explicit gay-sex scene between Mr. Darcy and Mr. Bingley, who are not just having sex but appear to be in a loving relationship. Herendeen gives some background to her decision in an essay included in the book, "The Story Behind *Pride/Prejudice*," in which she writes, regarding why authors include (hardcore) sex in their Austen fanfiction, "it's because we don't see sex as inherently sinful or disgusting that we can include it in adaptations of older works without regarding the new material as erotica or obscene."[61] Yet Wells, in investigating the reception of this more queer sex–filled fanfiction, found that mainstream readers (as opposed to those in queerer communities, such as Archive of Our Own or Autostraddle) didn't take to the sex depicted in the novel. Other readers, however, came to the aid of the author, sarcastically writing that "within P & P variations it seems to be easily accepted . . . [that Darcy] might be a werewolf, a vampire, a dragon, a ghost or a zombie hunter—but love a man—oh my, how gross!"[62] Another commenter offers the same point, sans sarcasm: "If Seth Grahame-Smith can introduce zombies into Jane Austen—adding novelty but offering no real insight on the original—why not [sex]?"[63] Our understanding of what type of sex was and was not appropriate (or is or is not appropriate) is still colored by our society. Although the queer community is much more visible than ever before, even in fiction some readers don't want to see queer sex. More for us!

Linda Berdoll and many, many others certainly fill the gap between queer sex in Austen and no sex at all. Berdoll is a fan of Austen, and the work, although professionally published like Pride/Prejudice (which even refers to itself as an alternative universe or AU, using the language of fanfiction in professionally published works[64]), would be at home on a platform such as Archive of Our Own or some of the locked Austen forums (those that would allow sex stories, anyway). Although being a published book, Berdoll's writing is rather reminiscent of the excerpts from "10 Lesbian Sex Scenes I Wrote Before I Had Lesbian Sex." The dichotomy between Austen's closed-vest writing and the nakedly unashamed porn might be titillating according to Roger Sales, but for many readers it can be a jarring experience. Sometimes it's better to think of these as faux Austen, rather than as Austen continuations, as Austen's style is notoriously difficult to ape.

The New York Times reported an article that discussed the word choices made by Austen and how the words she wrote, literally, affect how difficult it is to copy her style. Austen's works sit in their own little bubble outside of all the other major literary periods and genres. She stayed far from words along the physical side of things (close, empty, round, shoulder, watch, etc.)[65] and medieval words (blood, cast, death, fierce, herbs, foul, etc.)[66] while using more words that are abstract (desire, favor, gratitude) and the most words from the category of emotion and time (fortnight, sorry, suppose, very, week, glad, etc.). But what sets her the most apart linguistically is that she uses intensifying words more than other authors (so, very, much), words which lend themselves to irony, which Austen specialized in. The problem? Sex scenes, especially those that are hardcore, heartfelt, or explicit, are rarely written with irony. They could be *read* with irony, but they aren't written to be read as such.

Trying to fit in scenes like the following with Austen's reserved, ironic style can be a brain teaser.

> Because she had felt of his body in full cry, and therefore appreciated the ampleness of his . . . credentials, Elizabeth had harboured a certainty she would not be taken unawares when she saw them. Yet, she could not help but stare (by reason of its tumescence, his torch of love so happened to be trained directly upon her and it was difficult to disregard). When she finally wrested her eyes from thence, she raised one eyebrow slightly as if to question the viability of what nature insisted was, indeed, possible. In that he sought refuge from her gaze beneath the counter-pane with considerable dispatch, she concluded that her dumbfounded expression was less subtle than she hoped.
>
> Her attention to passion, however, was reclaimed from the distraction of the size of his instrument for it forthwith. For he commenced to industriously explore beneath her gown.[67]

These sex-insert fics might be hot as heck, might explore the bisexual nature of characters, or queer characters, or might just provide authors, readers, and fans with some fun sexy times for the characters they love, but perhaps they're best read as stories from another era rather than trying to mesh with Austen's style.

Audiences can connect with anything as long as there is a hook for them to hold onto. Sometimes, though, the hook isn't a longing stare between Elizabeth and Darcy but between Emma and Harriet or Darcy and Bingley. Sometimes a longing stare isn't enough. Fans need to be able to connect, to find that entry point, even if they have to create it themselves from subtext. Identity, sex, sexuality, and representation can get all folded up and twisted around, but the fans are here to help make sure that what does get to new fans and new readers is something that they can hold onto, engorged or not.

8

Lady Susan? Bisexual?
It's More Likely Than You'd Think

ZOE

Bisexual stereotypes in media: ~free love~ manic pixie dream folks, chaotic forces of nature driven largely by libido, I don't like labels sweaty ;))

Bisexual stereotypes among actual bisexuals: fucking useless but probably wearing a cool jacket

—@callmekitto on Twitter

Lady Susan is bisexual.

I know, I know, that's not a provable statement, even from the canon original text. But I'm making the statement anyway. The Lady Susan depicted in *Love & Friendship* (2016) (Whit Stillman's adaptation of *Lady Susan*) is bisexual. She's in love with both her friend and confidante Alicia Johnson and her paramour Mr. Manwaring.

In the previous chapter I discussed the fact that folks who point out LGBTQ+ ships in works aren't expecting them to come true. With content such as television or in ongoing media like podcasts and book/graphic novel series, there's always the *hope* (only sometimes fulfilled) that a queer relationship will be recognized, but we are always seeing them where they are *implied* to be. To quote myself: "The shipping, the act itself, uses the complexity found outside of straightforward storytelling (pun intended) and injects 'how people struggle to allow themselves what they want.'"[1] Lady Susan and Alicia Johnson struggle to be around one another consistently, and in the film adaptation they mourn their separation more than Lady Susan mourns anything else.

There is always the question of "so what" that comes up when someone like myself—a fan, an academic, and also a queer woman—attempts to show the queerness of an otherwise "obviously" straight character. It *is* true that lesbian or woman loving–woman sex was not recognized as real in the life of Jane Austen,[2] but that doesn't mean that those relationships didn't exist. It's true that Lady Susan ends up with, technically, two men, by the end of the novella, but that also doesn't negate the possibility of Lady Susan also at minimum yearning for Alicia Johnson. As scholars and as fans we are *experts* at reading between the lines. We understand subtext and we understand that not all people are going to see the same thing in subtext. But that doesn't mean the subtext isn't there. The makers of the film *Love & Friendship* marketed the film with two women looking longingly at each other in three of four posters and included one woman looking longingly at another in the fourth. In the world of subtext that's barely *sub*text. It's practically text.

Lady Susan longs to be with her friend Alicia Johnson, but Lady Susan is clearly at least in a relationship, if not also in love, with Mr. Manwaring. In *Love & Friendship* the abrupt ending of the canon *Lady Susan* is extended and softened slightly, showing Mr. Manwaring living with Lady Susan and Sir James Martin, her new husband. Lady Susan is pregnant! With Mr. Manwaring's child. They are, clearly, committed to one another. And so, as the audience, we see the conflict: Susan loves her dear friend Alicia, but the trappings of society, her own need (and desire) for a specific standard of living, and the necessity of providing for her daughter prevent her from crossing that particular line. She marries for propriety and continues her affair with Mr. Manwaring for pleasure and (possibly) love, but her love for Alicia Johnson lives on, and so Whit Stillman's version of Lady Susan is bisexual.

Interestingly, the first time I noticed that Lady Susan might be portrayed as bisexual was when I saw the posters for the film when it premiered at the 2016 Sundance Festival. The advertisements for the premier showing and the poster released after Sundance both have Alicia Johnson and Lady Susan portrayed prominently together. In the poster released before the premier, in fact, it is *only* Lady Susan and Alicia Johnson, looking at each other with a knowing and warm look, with the text "A lady never reveals her tactics."[3] Although Alicia, as Lady Susan's closest friend, is a regular presence in the film, she does not take up so much screen time that I expected her to be pictured with Lady Susan on the promotional poster. So I wondered if we were to assume that they were *also* in love, along with Lady Susan being in love/lust with Mr. Manwaring.

In France, and later in the United States, another poster showed up as the promotional train continued, also prominently featuring Alicia Johnson. This time? Alicia and Lady Susan walk away from a man (Reginald De Courcy), who watches them. Alicia and Lady Susan, though, have eyes only for each other. Yet another poster, first in the UK, then in the US, from later that year, after Sundance, featured Lady Susan looking out into the camera, and both Alicia Johnson and Reginald De Courcy slightly behind her, looking at her, the same way two rivals are positioned on a typical romantic-comedy DVD cover. Alicia Johnson, for those counting along, had been in the front-and-center romantic view of Lady Susan in *three* posters thus far. In fact, it's not until the final release of the movie that a poster/cover pops up that doesn't centrally feature the two women together. Instead, it pictures Lady Susan, in a stunning, coquettish hat, looking out at the camera and the two male rivals standing behind her, looking at her. But wait. In the background, in a carriage, sits Alicia Johnson—also looking at Lady Susan longingly.[4]

And look—I've been tricked before. The marketing for movies and TV shows often plays up relationships and moments that are fleeting or even nonexistent in the final film, but these posters held promise, since I'd read the novella and as a scholar I knew the theoretical potential for woman-loving-woman romance. And as a fan I longed for it. So let's take a look at the film, shall we?

Just four minutes and twelve seconds into the movie we meet Mrs. Alicia Johnson, before we meet Lady Susan's daughter or even Lady Susan herself. Only thirty seconds later we find out that Alicia Johnson has been forbidden from seeing Lady Susan. They have to meet in secret, in carriages, or while Mr. Johnson (Alicia's older, middle-aged husband) is out of the house—they are essentially having an affair. The *reason* for his ruling is Lady Susan's, shall we say, outward affair with Mr. Manwaring, as well as her coquettish nature, which has caused scandal.[5] Most of Lady Susan's screen time shows her attempting to manipulate others into doing her bidding, but the majority of the time spent with Alicia Johnson is attempting to mold their lives together again and return some normalcy to their relationship. When Lady Susan comes to visit London after her daughter Frederica runs away from school, Alicia and Lady Susan walk together and discuss the best ways to convince Frederica to stay in school. Alicia has helped Lady Susan keep Sir James Martin in love with Frederica. Alicia ferries notes, does Lady Susan's bidding, even risks being sent back to Connecticut (her worst nightmare, as a Royalist) by spending time with Lady Susan. They confer and confide, squirreling away time in carriages and on walks, and my bisexual heart began to sing. They were so clearly in a long-term comfortable *relationship*, to my eyes.

During one of their clandestine liaisons Lady Susan is talking with Alicia Johnson about not letting Frederica come to Churchill, where Lady Susan is staying and where she is attempting to woo Reginald De Courcy. They have the following conversation:

> Alicia: That's wise.
> Lady Susan: What do you mean?
> A: The nearness of their ages, her and Reginald's.
> LS: Oh, how unkind.
> A: Forgive me.
> LS: [with a smile] Forgiven.
> Both: smile warmly at one another and lean toward each other[6]

The closeness of their banter, along with the ability to comment on one another's sexual history and physical appearance, indicates a closeness that Lady Susan does not have with anyone else—and also sounds startlingly like an "old timey" version of language you'd hear in a film such as *Mean Girls* ("Boo, you whore" or "Get in, loser, we're going shopping"[7]) or of the now-defunct Vine, "I love you, bitch."[8] These quotes represent language that women and couples use *today* to indicate closeness with gentle insults and instant forgiveness. The language indicates a comfort and intimacy that is almost never seen even between deeply close platonic or familial women elsewhere in Austen, in my experience. Even when Elizabeth and Jane share a bed and secrets in the 2005 *Pride and Prejudice* adaptation, this felt different, as the character of Lady Susan was so clearly comfortable around Alicia in a way she is only comfortable around one other, her known lover Mr. Manwaring.

In the scene directly following, when Alicia and Lady Susan are discussing Frederica and Reginald, Lady Susan is seen singing Alicia's virtues, telling Reginald, the man that she is attempting to marry, that "though even the best-bred Americans don't sound particularly fine, there's a freshness to her manner that I find particularly tonic."[9] Consistently, other than her domination of Reginald and her sex with (and possibly love of) Manwaring, Lady Susan finds men to be rather dull. In most instances she prefers to be around women of wit and power, and with so few in the story equal to her, Alicia Johnson is her only solace. In fact, later in the film, after Alicia has helped distract Reginald from Lady Susan and Mr. Manwaring's tête-à-tête, Lady Susan extolls Alicia's virtues once again, even using Alicia's friendship with her as a way to continue to gain favor with Reginald, as she holds Alicia in a high-enough regard that Lady Susan is willing to use her as a watermark for personality and poise.[10] The only two people for whom Lady Susan has a consistently positive word are Mr. Manwaring and Alicia Johnson. Even when she has positive comment about others in her life—Reginald, for instance—the comments are always tinged with a way to counteract the compliment. But with Mr. Manwaring and Alicia Johnson, the comments are consistently positive—a rarity indeed for Lady Susan.

Before I continue with the next paragraph, I'd like to insert a comment: I don't think that there are or should be traditionally "male" and "female" roles in a relationship today, but looking *historically* there were, including both at the time Austen was writing and the time Whit Stillman set *Love & Friendship*, so I am relying on those understood boundaries here.

Not quite related to Lady Susan being bisexual, but in the same vein as gender politics in general, around Alicia Johnson Lady Susan acts as most Austen male characters do. As YouTube book reviewer MercysBookishMusings points out,[11] Lady Susan is much more actively chasing the objects of her affection, who range from Reginald De Courcy to Sir James Martin to Mr. Manwaring, and in those scenes with her friend and confidante where they meet in secret to find ways to stay close to one another, Lady Susan also chases after Alicia Johnson, writing her letters and coordinating where and when to clandestinely meet. Emma, of Austen's *Emma*—in the fan community often regarded and interpreted as a lesbian[12]—also takes on the "male role" in her organizing of other people's lives but is rebuked for it. Mary Crawford, too, fits this type (and is also often seen in the fan community as queer in some cases[13]). In Lady Susan's case, as MercysBookishMusings adds, Lady Susan takes on the "male" role with Alicia Johnson as her partner in more than just attempting to woo her and stay around her. They plan for the future of Frederica *together*, with Lady Susan acting as the distant male figure rather than as a loving mother.[14] Alicia helps Lady Susan find a school and keep Frederica in Sir James Martin's mind, as a part of this woman-loving-woman partnership.

Interestingly, with almost no exception Alicia takes on the traditional "woman role" and agrees with and believes Lady Susan all the time. Lady Susan herself holds this kind of commitment and loyalty to be paramount to a relationship, telling Alicia of Reginald, "If he held me in true regard he would not believe such insinuations in my disfavor. A worthy lover should assume one has unanswerable motives for all one does."[15] The only two people for whom this is true in Lady Susan's life? Alicia Johnson and Mr. Manwaring: her closest and most treasured friend—and her lover. Along with always agreeing with Lady Susan, Alicia Johnson goes out of her way to help her friend, and Lady Susan always knows she can rely on Alicia. When she risks having her fiancé, Reginald, run into her paramour, Mr. Manwaring, Alicia steps in to distract Reginald for the evening. Unfortunately, Alicia faces the punishment for their affair as well. When Reginald hears the contents of a private letter, Mr. Johnson punishes Alicia for her continued contact with Lady Susan. Not her *role* in arranging the affair with Lady Susan and Mr. Manwaring, but the active contact between Alicia and Lady Susan, as it is an affair of their own. After all, between correspondence marked private, and secret meetings in carriages and on walks, the similarities between Lady Susan's affair with Mr. Manwaring and Lady Susan's affair with Alicia are striking.

But Lady Susan can steal moments where she and Alicia match wits and minds together. Their language increasingly becomes the language of lovers, Lady Susan telling Alicia, "I'm so glad you could steal away," and Alicia responding, "We can only meet through such subterfuges."[16] And more and more often, when Alicia asks about Lady Susan's attempted wooing of Reginald, her face and body posture indicate jealousy that Lady Susan is spending her attentions elsewhere. Alicia tells Lady Susan that no one really deserves her, but the implication, and the way that Alicia tenses her jaw and the long look that Lady Susan sends her way as Alicia keeps talking, implies that the end of that sentence isn't that the "young De Courcy is worth having"[17] but rather that no one really deserves Lady Susan but Alicia.

Toward the end of the film, but before Lady Susan is married, Alicia and Lady Susan meet for what Alicia says is their last time. Her husband has threatened her with moving to Connecticut (the colonies!) full time in order to complete his business there. Lady Susan tells her dear friend, "I had a feeling that the great word 'respectable' would someday divide us. Your husband I abhor, but we must yield to necessity. Our affection cannot be impaired by it, and in happier times when your situation is as independent as mine, we will again unite. For this I will impatiently wait."[18] During this speech Alicia looks more and more teary-eyed, her eyes slightly red as she considers a life without Lady Susan. And Lady Susan, for her part, is actually genuine in her affection for Alicia; the airs she puts on around her in-laws now disappear in the small carriage she shares with her friend, a sad smile on her face.

In a fascinating moment, the carriage slows as their conversation comes to an end and one paramour is exchanged for another as Mr. Manwaring approaches the carriage and the camera cuts away. Lady Susan's two loves come together.

After Lady Susan's marriage, all returns to the normalcy Alicia and Lady Susan have been craving. Alicia is allowed to be a part of Lady Susan's life again because Lady Susan has regained the respectability of a good marriage, and so Alicia and Lady Susan can carry on their affair, this time in the open, as female relationships were usually too unrecognized to be considered dangerous. When Alicia welcomes Sir James Martin, new husband of Lady Susan, she remarks, "There's a rightness to your being together. Not that any man could really deserve Lady Susan."[19] The comment is a double-edged sword: Sir James is stupid enough to let Lady Susan continue with her affairs, and so of course Alicia would favor their marriage and speak of their rightness in being together. And no *man* could truly deserve Lady Susan, because the deserving one is Alicia (and Mr. Manwaring, he of the exceptionally good looks).

To see LGBTQ+ characters in the material we read and watch and consume is not a fantasy. It is an understanding that people are not cardboard cutouts of traits and perceptions. Although we see these characters only briefly on the page or screen that doesn't mean that they don't, in their own world, have full lives. Books and movies and stories of all kinds are ways to look through the window of someone's life. It's true that they're *fictional* lives, but they are lives and most stories cover just a fraction of a life. This is where the fan and scholar can create and find more stories, whether through fanfiction or analysis, through art or text mining. For me, seeing Lady Susan's friendship with Alicia Johnson, it was obvious. They were in love and had resigned themselves to their heterosexual fates, but they knew and understood their love. A comfortable love a long time in the making, but more than platonic. It's all right that Lady Susan marries Sir James Martin and in the film is also pregnant with Mr. Manwaring's child—being in a straight-passing relationship does not negate bisexuality. Lady Susan can continue to love Alicia Johnson *and* Mr. Manwaring.

Where We Stand Now

Z: okie dokie

3 . . .

2 . . .

1 . . .

sent

H: JUST CLICK SEND

I CAN'T TAKE THE ANTICIPATION

Z: anticipating

antici

oh my god autocorrect ruined my rocky horror joke

H: Boo autocorrect

Uncultured swine

—Text conversation between Zoe and Holly as we submitted
the proposal for this book

It is doubtful, in the early 1800s, when a young Jane Austen sat at
her writing desk, that she imagined having the long-standing,
global impact that she has had. Which, of course not, unless she
somehow prophetically knew the internet was coming. And yet,
two hundred years later, her novels have become so much to so
many people. They are friends, sources of comfort, opportunities
to experience a romantic world of good manners and lovely dresses, witty and biting commentary on society. Her fans dress up and
travel to her home in England. They write and read stories based
on her novels and life. They overlay images from film adaptations
with ironic news headlines. They insert new characters (maybe
even themselves) or see romance where it may not have been explicitly intended. They laugh at Mr. Darcy being overcome by Elizabeth's ability to slay the undead. They tweet at Emma and Harriet,
or follow Cher Horowitz on social media. Somehow these biting
social commentaries have transcended almost every genre and

form of media, and fans keep taking what others offer and reimagining it tenfold. The Jane Austen fandom is truly astounding in its depth and breadth. The ability to build and interact with fan spaces online, where fans do not have to be physically in the same room or on the right mailing list to find and share content with other fans, has opened doors, windows, and hidden passages in the walls. Fans can find other fans with a few clicks or taps, can argue and critique, can create and consume an ever-expanding universe of content. It is remarkable to consider all that Austen fans have created, and to also realize: we are not done yet.

Zoe: Fandom is hard.

During the process of writing this book I watched a lot of *The Great British Bake Off/Great British Baking Show* on Netflix (procrastination is a beautiful thing). In one of the seasons a contestant named Kate is eliminated and she leaves good-naturedly, and in her exit interview she says that she's not going to stop baking but that she might not bake tomorrow.

That's me and fandom right now. I'm still in fandom, and I still love Austen. I'm still going to read fanfiction and argue about adaptations with friends and dive into arguments about what modern fandom is and is not . . . but maybe not tomorrow.

Investigating something you love or something that you are a part of is hard; it takes a lot out of you to willingly take a step back and say, "How can I critique this thing that I love," or "What is beyond what I usually perceive about this thing that I am a part of every day?" In college I decided that I wanted to do an independent study. I decided that I would read famous, and favorite, young adult books and analyze them. I drew up a syllabus, made my own assignments, got a professor on board, and jumped in. I had thought about texts critically before; I was a junior in college majoring in English and history, and in English I was focusing on Victorian novels. I *knew* how to engage critically with a text, how to do research . . . but I never had to do it for something I loved. Sure, I love Charles Dickens's books, especially *A Tale of Two Cities*, but that is different from *Harry Potter*, where the titular character and I literally grew up together. It was the first time I had to really dig into something I adored, the first time I had to engage with something that was a part of me and find fault with it. It was one of the hardest classes I ever took, and I did it to myself.

I did this book to myself, too.

The good news is that even though this book is the longest thing I've ever written and the longest project I've ever worked on, in some ways it was easier than deconstructing the flaws in *Harry Potter*. Although I *love* Jane Austen and have been involved in some capacity in the Austen fandom for quite some time, I lacked the historical context to engage with Austen's novels the same way that I engaged with *Discworld* or *Star Trek*. At age fifteen I was having arguments with a friend over the merits and demerits of Emma vs. Marianne, over whether the adaptations were better than the novels, but I wasn't as *emotionally* attached to Austen as I was to other worlds. And so, in a lot of ways, investigating the Austen fandom was fun! I was a lurker in the fandom, so I got to discover new pieces about this thing that I had admired for a long time. Austen and the Austen fandom are in some ways a rock for me—her texts aren't going to change, *Sense and Sensibility* isn't going to evaporate off my shelf, and I've discovered so much new stuff about Austen and cool continuations of her works, and honestly, I'm excited to reread her novels.

Investigating fandom, that was harder. As I talked about in our introduction, I have been either a part of fandom or on the periphery of fandom for a very, very long time. I was aware of what a Trekkie was before I was ten, and I was a part of the online *Harry Potter* fandom by age eleven. Fandom has waxed and waned in my life, just as my love for various media has, but in recent years, since graduate school, fandom has become a larger part of my life. I am a hockey fan (men's and women's), a fan of webcomics and books, a fan of TV shows and podcasts, and I'm active on Twitter, Tumblr, Reddit, Discord. . . . I even signed up for Pillowfort, a new (still in Beta as of October 2018) social media platform. I'm in so many DM groups on Twitter I sometimes can't keep track.

But fandom is full of flaws. When a group of people gather together to discuss something that they love it is inevitable that they are going to disagree about something. Now exponentially multiply the number of people involved in that disagreement. For some fandoms these days that can escalate into death threats against the author or other fans for creating works that don't line up with how others see the work. It can sometimes be Real People Fiction (RPF), which in turn can ruin real life friendships (I really do feel for the guys in One Direction). It can mean someone doxxing a sixteen-year-old for writing fanfiction about a ship pairing that someone doesn't like. These are all real things that I have witnessed in the past two years before and during writing this book, so I thought I was prepared to investigate the dark and dirty corners of Austen fandom. In some capacity I definitely was; I didn't find the same vitriol that I witnessed speeding across my Tumblr dashboard or Twitter timeline in the Voltron fandom or One Direction or anime, but there were uncomfortable parts that I realized I had participated in without knowing.

Austen fandom is stratified in a way I didn't expect it to be, although given my academic background, perhaps I should have. There're the academic fans, the Big Name Fans, and fan communities such as the Derbyshire Writers' Guild, where fan content has to be vetted by people who have claimed power, casual book fans, *and* casual movie fans, and these fandoms don't seem to get along. If someone hasn't read *Pride and Prejudice* but enjoys the movie, they get dumped on. And I recognized myself there—I've done that. But that's not fair: *Pride and Prejudice*, however fun and accessible to me, is not accessible to many, many people. It is written in a style that can be difficult to parse, it's long and complicated as a text, it's also a book, rather than a television show or a movie. There are fans who are physically or mentally never going to be able to read this piece of fiction in its canon state, let alone fans who simply don't enjoy reading that style or who find it boring, and that's okay—so why was I hating on them? They were still enjoying Austen's works in a different form. As I researched queer themes in Austen, or poked through blogs celebrating the great and wonderful Mr. Darcy aka Mr. Colin Firth, I realized that there was a lot of elitism that I had to give up both in fandom and in my own view of Austen and her works. And not just Austen, for me. Realizing the extent of the stratification of Austen fandom made me take a look at how I approached my other fandoms. Was I being actually inclusive? Was I welcoming? How was I encouraging or tearing down gatekeeping barriers? I am lucky that I started this deconstructing process early in the research for this book, but bad habits are a hard thing to give up; I am still working on it and will continue to work on it. I can say that I'm more welcoming, more open to new fandom concepts, more willing to engage with fans who don't fan in the same way I do. And I'm glad that the Austen fandom is out there, reminding me every day that stratification in fandom is still there, and still a problem, and that we can work hard to fix it in the Austen fandom and all other fandoms.

As for my views on Austen? We see Austen as this canonical writer of texts that you read in school and write stately papers about, but that's wrong. She's a satirist and a humorist and a master of observation comedy. She understands people! It took some time, but by the time I'm writing this, I can say that a lot of the elitism that I walked into this book with has gone. Austen should be for everyone, and that means adapting and changing and adjusting the stories . . . and that's okay. It's *good*. Researching fandom was exhausting, but it opened my eyes to some of my own issues with media and adaptations, and it helped me along the way, so maybe it's time for another book! (Or possibly a nap.)

Holly: It feels like falling in love for the first time . . . again.

While this was not my first go at critiquing literature that I love—I do have two degrees in English, after all—this is the first time I have truly grappled with what it means to be a fan and to participate in a fandom, especially one as dear to me as Jane Austen. I have been a fan, and have participated in some fan practices before, but I never truly considered how I personally straddle the line between fan and scholar and navigate these two sometimes contradictory worlds. The last time I spent a considerable amount of time critiquing one of Austen's novels, it took me years to be able to fully enjoy the book again. After spending a year in graduate school picking *Emma* and *Clueless* apart, some of the joy I once had for the novel was gone. I spent too much time and energy finding the flaws, and they overshadowed my original love of the novel. While I hadn't maintained a distance from being an Austen fan during the course of that work, I did take some time after completing graduate school to distance myself from at least that one text.

My work as a scholar did not diminish my enjoyment of all of Austen, however, and I spent the intervening years reading *Persuasion* and *Pride and Prejudice* again and again. (I like the others, but those two are by far my favorites.) I dove into spin-off series, and continuation novels, and of course, any film adaptation I could get my hands on. This time around feels different, though. Right now, I cannot wait to pick up one of her novels again. Delving into the depths of Austen fandom has renewed my vigor for reading the novels themselves. It feels like echoes of what Juliette Wells found when speaking with Austen fans for *Everybody's Jane*: participating in fan practices can foster a greater appreciation and understanding of the source text.[1] I may avoid doing anything but rolling around happily in her prose (maybe read or write a fanfic), but after spending so much time learning about how other people experience and enjoy Austen, I am anxious to dive in and enjoy her again myself—as just a fan—without the internal or external pressure to turn something I *love* into something I *do*. There are so many fun things happening in Austen fandom that I would probably never have encountered were it not for this book. I want to revel in the fandom experiences that we have uncovered. My family and friends seem anxious for that, too, since they keep sending me links for Jane Austen board games, card games, and computer games. One friend gave me a book called *A Guinea Pig Pride and Prejudice,* because why not? This experience has also, I think, made me less self-conscious about simply *enjoying* being a fan and participating in fan spaces. Before, I largely kept my obsession to myself—much like the heroine of *Austenland* hides her Colin Firth DVDs in her houseplant—I didn't want people knowing how many Austen films I had seen, much less owned. But now that I have discovered how wide the fan space is, how many of us are out there, and how much content there is to play with, I am ready to experience it all. Judge me if you dare.

While researching and writing this book did not uncover a lot of unexpected tension for me, I cannot say that I have at no time felt the pull of the scholar while reading or seeing fan content. In a sense, my unease in the Austen fandom stems not from a need to maintain a proper distance from that which I wish to study but from the dissonance between fans of the novels and fans of the films: I sometimes cannot stand when I see a quote from an Austen adaptation attributed to Austen herself. Not just to one of the novels, but to *Jane Austen*. I do feel a certain amount of possessiveness over people *getting things right* when it comes to quoting Austen's words. After the 2005 *Pride and Prejudice*, for example, which was widely seen and loved, and likely brought new people into the Austenverse, some fan-created works used quotes from the film that were not in the original novel, added them to images from the film, and list-ed "Jane Austen" as the source, rather than the film. Is this elitist of me? I am not judging them for enjoying the film—I love it myself—but I want Austen's prose to get the credit it deserves, and it is better than some of the film adap-tations make it out to be. I also tend to be defensive when people call Austen's novels love stories or romances, because even though the fan in me loves the happily-ever-afters of the romantic pairings, the literary critic in me wants to shout, *"But they're not romances! They are biting social commentary!"*

I imagine that the frustration I feel when faced with these types of misat-tributed quotes or the reduction of Austen's well-crafted irony to romance may be similar to how some scholars might feel when they see Austen fans dressing up in Regency gowns and attending balls. So I do experience a certain tension within my own dual roles as Austen fan and Austen schol-ar, though perhaps not in the traditional way. My contradictions are almost entirely encompassed within my fan experiences, and not between my fan and scholarly experiences. Being a fan of Austen brought me to studying her and her novels more intently, with a scholarly lens. While at times that can lessen the joy I take from the Austenverse, I keep coming back, as both fan and scholar. The two identities have become intertwined for me, so much that separating them out feels impossible. In fact, my Austen fandom is one of the only places I *don't* keep my aca-fan identity separated. I have a Tumblr, which uses a pseudonym, where I engage with other fans and content related to books, authors, shows, and films that I like. I don't put scholarly things on that blog. That blog is solely for me to find fan-created content and enjoy it. But Jane Austen? Her works and her persona straddle both the pop and schol-arly realms—so my interactions with her do, too.

In a way, writing this book and rediscovering Austen fandom has felt a bit like encountering Austen for the first time again: wide-eyed, swept away by the world and the characters. Since I was first introduced to Jane Austen as a high school senior, her novels have become not just some of my favorite books, but something that feels a bit like home. They have been companions for most of my life. Through every move, life event, tragedy, I have kept Aus-ten by my side. When my father passed away unexpectedly in 2016, I packed the very first Jane Austen novel I ever owned in my suitcase (*Pride and Prejudice*, naturally). I had no intention of reading it during the time I was traveling home for his funeral, but I knew that along with the necklace my dad gave me and a black dress, Austen needed to be with me as I faced one of the hardest things I would ever have to do. I didn't read it, either. I don't think I ever took it out of my suitcase, but it was there, and just having it with me felt a little like peace. And while I treasure this familiarity, this comfort like that from a life-long friend, I had forgotten how exciting that first discovery of a new author or novel can be: the rush and desire to devour every word. I feel that again, with an author I've been well acquainted with for upwards of fifteen years, and one I have critiqued and puzzled over. It has been unexpected, but exciting.

Where Do We Go from Here?

When Henry Jenkins chose to "out" himself as a fan in his book, *Textual Poachers*, he recalls the decision as being controversial.[2] Fan studies, still in its earliest days, drew heavily from ethnographic studies, where researchers were expected to remain outside of the communities they studied. While many researchers today enthusiastically and unashamedly embrace their fan identities as part of their scholarly selves, the notion that academics cannot be fans still persists. Therefore, our decision at the beginning of this text to situate ourselves as both fans and academics—indeed, to claim our fan identities as the *primary* space from which we're writing—has proven to be more complicated than we imagined. Not fully grasping the sharp lines drawn between these two spheres in the past, and the work that has been done since the advent of fan studies that has led to a blurring of those lines, we simply did not realize that the ways in which we situated our fannishness and our scholarly work were at all radical. For us, and for a new generation of fans, the ability to combine these two identities is simply second nature. We don't, as Jenkins describes it, feel "the need to defend the community," of the fandoms in which we participate, and of which we are also critical.[3]

This easy combination of academic and fan may be particularly facilitated by the nature of Austen fandom. Austen fans have always been stratified, from conservative politicians who clashed with progressive suffragettes in the early 1900s[4] to the film fans who broke off from the academic-controlled spheres in the mid-1990s. The Jane Austen of the fans has always coexist-ed alongside the Jane Austen of the literary canon, and neither sphere has stunted growth in the other. Fans are still playing in the sandbox, producers are still adapting films and plays, and scholars are still writing dissertations and books, often incorporating adaptations that start as fan ideas, like Whit Stillman's *Lady Susan* adaptation *Love & Friendship*. Perhaps the Austen fandom is proof that these intertwined experiences of a shared text can coexist, not in spite of the tension that exists between them, but *because of* the contra-dictory ways in which people read and do Austen-related work. It is through this interplay of academic and fan, book and film, fanfiction and profession-al adaptation, that the Austen fandom has continued to grow and created a space for a heightened experience for fans and academics alike. Perhaps there are those, on both sides of the divide, who will want still to assert a "right" or "wrong" way to view Austen, but we do not count ourselves among them—as academics or fans. We see and personally experience the value to both ways of being.

Jane Austen fandom is unique. It shares a long history with other liter-ary fandoms, like those of Shakespeare, Sherlock Holmes, and Don Quixo-te, but, especially in today's world, fans are more likely to encounter Austen first through a film or as pleasure reading than as required schoolwork. The nature of the fandom is amorphous—constantly in flux, ebbing and flowing as new material is added or new fans join the shared spaces. Austen fandom is full of contradictions: both popular and academic, both digital and ana-log, both grounded in texts and novels and in the mysterious persona of Jane Austen herself. It is a fandom that grew with so few source texts but that has managed to find and create endless ways of being and doing, and has adapt-ed to new ways of being a fan, seemingly effortlessly. We've no doubt it will continue, and that fans will, like Austen herself, push boundaries and shatter ceilings.

Notes

INTRODUCTION

1. Many other terms appeared, including mentions of specific characters or novels.

2. Henry Jenkins, *Textual Poachers: Television Fans and Participatory Culture* (New York: Routledge, 2012), 4–7. Jenkins discusses this tension in many of his works, noting how his own identity as a fan complicates his academic discourse on fan communities and cultures.

3. See chapter 3.

4. Henry Jenkins, "Acafandom and Beyond: Week Two, Part Two," Confessions of an Aca-Fan (ser.), *Henry Jenkins* (blog), accessed May 14, 2018, http://henry jenkins.org/blog/2011/06/acafandom_and_beyond_week_two_1.html.

5. Henry Jenkins, *Fans, Bloggers, and Gamers* (New York: New York University Press, 2006), 11.

6. Devoney Looser, *The Making of Jane Austen* (Baltimore: Johns Hopkins University Press, 2017).

7. Looser, 181.

8. Looser, 218.

9. Claudia L. Johnson, *Jane Austen's Cults and Cultures* (Chicago: University of Chicago Press), 8. "Janeite" is a term used to refer to Jane Austen fans who are considered obsessive or maniacal. It first appeared in 1894. Other, more scholarly fans sometimes prefer the term "Austenite."

10. I would like to note that I am a to-the-end Buffy and Angel shipper, but Spike had such a bad-boy appeal to my teenage self, and I loved their complicated chemistry.

11. NautiBitz, "In Heat," Nocturnal Light, 2007, http://spikeluver.com/Spuffy Realm/viewstory.php?sid=28212. I should have known that with an author's name like that I was in for something more than PG-rated.

12. "Fancasting" is when a fan of a particular piece of media, most often written, will create a "dream cast" of who he/she would like to see play the role of certain characters in a film or television adaptation. "Shipping wars" refers

to factions of fans who support one romantic pairing ("relationshipping") and may disagree with others' preferred romantic pairings.

13. A storytelling technique that incorporates different kinds of media through which the story is told, such as using a combination of videos, blogs, and social media.

14. My first actual foray into fan Twitter or Tumblr came with *How To Train Your Dragon 2* (2014). I had been happily, if passively, following (various) fandom blogs for a while, but never on social media. I have now become deeply involved, if passively, in multiple fandoms on both Twitter and Tumblr, ranging from real hockey to a hockey webcomic to the DCTV universe, and, of course, Austen.

15. A fan creation that combines multiple fandoms into a single creative work. These can take the form of gifsets, fanfiction, image edits, quotes, screenshots, and so on.

16. Abbreviation for "Massive Multiplayer Online Role Playing Game," where players assume the identity of a character (original or canon), usually represented by an avatar, and play through a story or series of scenes, making decisions and acting as they believe their character would.

17. Johnson, 8.

18. Johnson, 44.

19. This is why Austen's novels were often given to war-scarred soldiers to treat shell shock, as PTSD was known at the time, as noted in Johnson, 102.

20. A portmanteau of *fan* and *canon*, "fanon" is used to refer to fan-created ideas or tropes that have been accepted officially as part of the fan community.

21. The first *Bridget Jones's* film (2001) even takes the Colin-Firth-as-Mr.-Darcy trope one step further, with the actor appearing in the Darcy-inspired role.

22. Laura Stampler, "This Picture of Benedict Cumberbatch as Mr. Darcy Will Make the World a Better Place," *Time*, September 16, 2016, accessed June 18, 2018, http://time.com /3386696/benedict-cumberbatch-mr-darcy.

23. Johnson, 8.

24. An original piece of writing based on an existing text, character, or world, written by a fan. Historically a writer is not paid for access to his or her work, although there have been recent debates around the monetization of fan work.

25. Eric Schulmiller, " 'Shipping' and the Enduring Appeal of Rooting for Love," *Atlantic*, December 27, 2014, http://www.theatlantic.com/entertainment/archive/2014/12/ shipping-and-the-enduring-appeal-of-rooting-for-love/383954.

26. Johnson, 99–126.

27. Jane Austen Society of the United Kingdom, http://www.janeaustensoci.freeuk.com.

28. Jane Austen Society of North America, last modified November 30, 2016, http://jasna.org.

29. This video was featured on a past AGM page, but as of this writing, it is currently unavailable.

30. K. Mirmohamadi, *The Digital Afterlives of Jane Austen: Janeites at the Keyboard* (New York: Palgrave Macmillan, 2014).

31. Anne Jamison, *Fic: Why Fanfiction Is Taking Over the World* (Dallas: BenBella Books, 2013), 42.

32. Regina Jeffers, "Austen Fandom vs. Austen Academics, a Guest Post from Melanie Rachel," *Austen Authors* (blog), November 19, 2017, https://austenauthors.net/austen-fandom-vs-austen-academics-a-guest-post-from-melanie-rachel.

33. Mel Stanfill, "'They're Losers, but I Know Better': Intra-Fandom Stereotyping and the Normalization of the Fan Subject," *Critical Studies in Media Communication* 30, no. 2 (June 1, 2013): 117–34, https://doi.org/10.1080/15295036.2012.755053.

34. *Pride and Prejudice*, 1938, IMDB, http://www.imdb.com/title/tt0414386/?ref_=nv_sr_8.

35. "Lady Susan Facsimile," March 20, 2014, http://www.themorgan.org/collection/jane-austen/lady-susan.

36. "Jane Austen in Popular Culture," Wikipedia, last modified Febuary 17, 2018, https://en.wikipedia.org/wiki/Jane_Austen_in_popular_culture#Film_and_television.

37. "Ever, Jane: The Virtual World of Jane Austen," MMORPG, accessed February 19, 2018, http://www.everjane.com.

38. Although memes have a long history, we are defining them as images, often with superimposed text and/or short text snippets that circulate through the zeitgeist and can be applied to many situations and fandoms.

39. Hashtags are a system of categorizing and organizing posts on social media sites by preceding a word or phrase with #. It can also be used to add commentary or captions that the writer does not want to include in the primary post text.

40. *Sherlock Holmes* and Arthur Conan Doyle provide a nice example of the opposite. Doyle became so tired of writing *Holmes* stories that he sometimes simply published fan-mailed stories instead of his own. Jamison, *Fic*, 43.

41. *Harry Potter* and J. K. Rowling bucked this trend when Rowling encouraged fanworks. She was among the first modern authors to publicly do so, and many others (including *Twilight*'s author Stephenie Meyer) followed suit (Jamison, 96.) *Star Trek* and Anne Rice, however, have a much more tumultuous relationship with their fans.

CHAPTER 1

1. A fan who is well known in their particular fandom and can often be looked to as a guide or gatekeeper.

2. Aja Romano, "Canon, Fanon, Shipping and More: A Glossary of the Tricky Terminology That Makes Up Fandom," Vox, June 7, 2016, http://www.vox.com/2016/6/7/11858680/fandom-glossary-fanfiction-explained.fd.

3. Tanya Erzen, *Fanpire: The Twilight Saga and the Women Who Love It* (Boston: Beacon Press, 2012), 122.

4. Aja Romano, "Edgar Allan Poe Is Uniting All Your 2016 Social Phobias in One Surprisingly Durable Meme," Vox, October 14, 2016, http://www.vox.com/2016/10/14/13274974/tumblr-cask-of-amontillado-meme.

5. Danette Chavez, "Chris Evans Won't Stop Fighting Real-Life Supervillain Donald Trump," AV/News, March 15, 2017, accessed April 30, 2017, http://www.avclub.com/article/chris-evans-wont-stop-fighting-real-life-supervill-252129.

6. A good example of this can be found in this headline about Daniel Radcliffe: Kyle Smith, "Harry Potter Plays a Farting Dead Man in New Movie," *New York Post* Entertainment, January 23, 2016, http://nypost.com/2016/01/23/harry-potter-plays-a-farting-dead-man-in-new-movie.

7. "FAQ," Pemberley Digital, accessed January 29, 2017, http://www.pemberleydigital.com/emma-approved/faq.

8. "Where Do Emma's Videos Exist in World?," Pemberley Digital, accessed January 29, 2017, http://www.pemberleydigital.com/where-do-emmas-videos-exist-in-world.

9. "Where Do Emma's Videos Exist in World?"

10. Too long; didn't read.

11. Katie Buenneke, "Why *Emma Approved* Didn't Work as Well as *The Lizzie Bennet Diaries* Did," *LA Weekly*, April 7, 2014, http://www.laweekly.com/arts/why-emma-approved-didnt-work-as-well-as-the-lizzie-bennet-diaries-did-4499200.

12. As of October 25, 2018.

13. Kimiko De Freytas-tamura, "Mr. Darcy, You're No Colin Firth," *New York Times*, February 9, 2017, https://www.nytimes.com/2017/02/09/books/colin-firth-mr-darcy.html.

14. Which have all followed the dark-haired, broad-chested, square-jawed model based on the casting of each successive Mr. Darcy, as can be seen in the gifset presented here: http://halfagony-halfhope.tumblr.com/post/122544585196/darcy-and-elizabeth-second-proposal.

15. Because there are no archived images of the 1938 televised live-to-TV adaptation of *Pride and Prejudice* this information about stature/looks is pulled from images of Andrew Osborn in a later film, *Poet's Pub*.

16. Although the physical nature of Colin Firth's Mr. Darcy is still attractive according to the beauty standards of the 2010s, it's interesting to note that this applies to the first filmed Mr. Darcy as well. Although beauty standards have changed drastically for women in the intervening years, either fans are married to a brunet, barrel-chested Mr. Darcy or beauty standards for men haven't changed as much. This isn't something we'll dive into, but it's interesting to note.

17. "The Real Mr Darcy—A Dramatic Re-Appraisal," *Pride and Prejudice*, Drama UKTV, February 9, 2017, http://drama.uktv.co.uk/pride-and-prejudice/article/real-mr-darcy-dramatic-re-appraisal.

18. Alanna Bennett, "Community Post: What A 'Racebent' Hermione Granger Really Represents," BuzzFeed Community, accessed March 21, 2017, http://www.buzzfeed.com/alannabennett/what-a-racebent-hermione-granger-really-represen-d2yp.

19. Technically, the 1958 *Pride and Prejudice* was aired on the BBC but not produced by them, but it counts toward this total as the BBC distribution counts as dedication of Jane Austen adaptations. "Jane Austen in Popular Culture," Wikipedia, last modified February 17, 2018, https://en.wikipedia.org/w/index.php?title=Jane_Austen_in_popular_culture&oldid=770874300.

20. Deborah Cartmell, *Screen Adaptations: Jane Austen's Pride and Prejudice: The Relationship between Text and Film* (London: Methuen Drama, 2010), 67.

21. Cartmell, 69.

22. "Bing Lee and His 500 Teenage Prostitutes," *The Lizzie Bennet Diaries*, YouTube video, April 9, 2012, https://www.youtube.com/watch?v=2KjOskZJEAc. This is a good example of a fanfiction piece referencing Colin Firth as Mr. Darcy in an easter egg version for fans to find and understand.

23. mithrandir, "Firthing," Urban Dictionary, August 27, 2013, http://www.urbandictionary.com/define.php?term=Firthing.

24. Cartmell, 74–76.

25. Cartmell, 96.

26. Anton Kessler, " 'I've Been Cursed by Darcy,' Says Firth," Daily Mail.com, accessed April 17, 2017, http://www.dailymail.co.uk/tvshowbiz/article-136939/Ive-cursed-Darcy-says-Firth.html.

27. Cartmell, 104.

28. Cartmell, 133.

29. All comment quotes from "Spy Drama Star Is 'New Mr Darcy,'" BBC News Entertainment, June 14, 2005, http://news.bbc.co.uk/2/hi/entertainment/3797535.stm.

30. "Star Takes Pride in New Prejudice," BBC News Entertainment, September 5, 2005, http://news.bbc.co.uk/2/hi/entertainment/4180324.stm.

31. "Spy Drama Star Is 'New Mr Darcy.'"

32. Not as much undress as originally planned, though. According to numerous interviews, Colin Firth confirmed that originally the script called for him to be totally nude. Colette Fahy, "I Was Meant to Be Wearing Nothing," Mail Online, updated January 23, 2015, http://www.dailymail.co.uk/tvshowbiz/article-2922738/Colin-Firth-says-meant-wearing-famous-Pride-Prejudice-lake-scene.html.

33. Nicholas Barber, "Pride and Prejudice at 20: The Scene That Changed Everything," September 22, 2015, *Culture* (blog), BBC, http://www.bbc.com/culture/story/20150922-pride-and-prejudice-at-20-the-scene-that-changed-everything.

34. Nate Jones, "You May Enjoy This Photo of Benedict Cumberbatch Dressed as Mr. Darcy," *Vulture* (blog), *New York Magazine*, September 16, 2014, http://www.vulture.com/2014/09/benedict-cumberbatch-dressed-as-mr-darcy.html.

35. Which, honestly, to both of the authors of this book, looks a bit like a Zombie Mr. Darcy emerging from the depths to eat brains.

36. Liz Bury, "Mr Darcy Surfaces as Statue in London Lake," *Guardian*, July 8, 2013, accessed February 24, 2017, https://www.theguardian.com/books/2013/jul/08/mr-darcy-statue-pride-and-prejudice.

37. Jennifer Schuessler, "Mr. Darcy's Shirt Is Coming to America," *New York Times*, March 8, 2016, https://www.nytimes.com/2016/03/09/arts/television/mr-darcys-shirt-is-coming-to-america.html.

38. Stories, usually short or snippets, that expand on an agreed-upon or canon aspect of a character or story.

39. Barber.

40. Otavia Propper, friend and editor, pointed out the prescriptive vs. descriptive definition.

41. Scholars, sure, but there's a constant tension between scholars and fans.

42. "About Us," The Republic of Pemberley, accessed May 18, 2017, http://pemberley.com/?page_id=11874.

43. Crysty, "Contributor Guidelines **PLEASE READ BEFORE POSTING**," Derbyshire Writ-

ers Guild June 23, 2008, accessed May 18, 2017, https://www.dwiggie.com/phorum/read
.php?5,2413,2413#msg-2413.

44. There are organizations that could function as BNFs and gatekeepers: JASNA (Jane Austen Society of North America), for example, and regional/local chapters thereof cross the boundary between scholar and fan and police what is and isn't acceptable at their conferences and in their papers.

45. Defined as "(a) a group of digital items sharing common characteristics of content, form, and/or stance; (b) that were created with awareness of each other; and (c) were circulated, imitated, and/or transformed via the internet by many users." Limor Shifman, *Memes in Digital Culture* (Cambridge, MA: MIT Press, 2014), 7–8.

46. Shifman, 9–10.

47. Romano.

48. This final line comes in a variety of forms, but boils down to this basic idea. Person A and Person B are usually personalized, and Person A is usually described as "me, on a date" and Person B as "them" or "you." See "Breadsticks," Know Your Meme, http://knowyourmeme.com/memes/breadsticks.

49. "Breadsticks Meme," Tumblr, accessed March 12, 2017. https://www.tumblr.com/search/breadsticks%20meme.

50. "Me, on a Date," *Off with the Fairies* (blog), Tumblr, accessed May 8, 2017, http://lovnlife.tumblr.com/post/125763112635/me-on-a-date-so-have-you-read-pride-and.

51. Shifman, 81–82.

52. "Beautiful Cinnamon Roll Too Good for This World, Too Pure," Onion, January 23, 2014, accessed April 17, 2017, http://www.theonion.com/article/beautiful-cinnamon-roll-too-good-for-this-world-to-35038.

53. Other versions included "sinnamon roll," implying that the character was bad, or "burnt cinnamon roll, too bad for this world, too jaded," etc. "Beautiful Cinnamon Roll Too Good For This World, Too Pure," Know Your Meme, accessed March 12, 2017. http://knowyourmeme.com/memes/beautiful-cinnamon-roll-too-good-for-this-world-too-pure.

54. "Pride and Prejudice/The Onion Headlines : Period Dramas," Tumblr, accessed March 12, 2017, http://whatwouldelizabethbennetdo.tumblr.com/post/119094313870/pride-and-prejudicethe-onion-headlines.

55. Kahler, KC. "Austen + The Onion Masterpost," Tumblr, accessed March 12, 2017, https://kcinpa.tumblr.com/post/129726481568/austen-the-onion-masterpost.

56. Natalie Neill, "Gothic Parody," in *Romantic Gothic: An Edinburgh Companion*, ed. Angela Wright and Dale Townshend (Edinburgh: Edinburgh University Press, 2016), 185.

57. Neill, 192, 197, 199.

58. Tim Robey, "Love & Friendship Shows Just How Funny Jane Austen Can Be—Review," *Telegraph*, May 26, 2016, http://www.telegraph.co.uk/films/2016/05/26/love—friendship -shows-just-how-funny-jane-austen-can-be—-revie.

59. KC Kahler, "KC in PA—Austen + The Onion Masterpost," Tumblr, accessed May 18, 2017, https://kcinpa.tumblr.com/post/125781551483/kcinpa-via-austen-onion-headlines; screenshot of *Northanger Abbey* (2007), with the text "I'm Refreshingly Naive" superimposed over the right-hand side of the image.

60. KC Kahler, "KC in PA—Pride and Prejudice 2005 + Onion Headlines, Part . . . ." Tumblr, accessed March 12, 2017. http://kcinpa.tumblr.com/post/122885430458/pride-and-preju dice-2005-onion-headlines-part."

61. Sense and Spontaneity, "Dear Mr Darcy," YouTube video, May 4, 2017, https://www.you -tube.com/watch?v=ekVdhO7P4Nw.

62. Sense and Spontaneity, 2:25.

63. paintmegolden, "Dancing with Our Hands Tied," Tumblr, *Dancing with Our Hands Tied* (blog), May 30, http://paintmegolden.tumblr.com/post/161252842758/next-up-in-line-for- queer-jane-austen-adaptations.

64. Anton Kessler, "Telling Men on Dating Sites about How I'm Convinced Charlotte Lucas Is a Lesbian Is How I'm Spending My Night. #NoRegrets," Tweet, @*amitygardens* (blog), July 10, 2017, https://twitter.com/amitygardens/status/883148040579817472.

65. "AUSTEN Jane—Works," Archive of Our Own, accessed November 12, 2017, http://archi- veofourown.org/works?utf8=%E2%9C%93&commit=Sort+and+Filter&work_search%5B sort_column%5D=revised_at&work_search%5Bcategory_ids%5D%5B%5D=116&work_ search%5Bother_tag_names%5D=&work_search%5Bquery%5D=&work_search%5Blan guage_id%5D=&work_search%5Bcomplete%5D=0&tag_id=AUSTEN+Jane+-+Works.

CHAPTER 2

1. *Clueless*, directed by Amy Heckerling (1995; Los Angeles, CA: Paramount Pictures, 1999), DVD.

2. Martha Rampton, "Four Waves of Feminism," Pacific University Oregon, October 25, 2015, https://www.pacificu.edu/about/media/four-waves-feminism.

3. Jeff Benjamin, "Why Iggy Azalea Recreated 'Clueless' for her 'Fancy' Video," Fuse, ac- cessed February 5, 2018, https://www.fuse.tv/videos/2014/05/iggy-azalea-fancy-clueless -interview.

4. Jessica Blankenship and Ella Cerón, "Present Day Clueless," Twitter, accessed February 23, 2018, https://twitter.com/ModernClueless.

5. See chapter 1 for more insight into meme culture, as well as how Austen fans use memes to interact with each other and those outside the fandom.

CHAPTER 3

1. Qtd. in Laura Miller, "You Belong to Me: The Fanfiction Boom Is Reshaping the Power Dynamics between Creators and Consumers," *Vulture* (blog), *New York Magazine*, March 11, 2015, http://www.vulture.com/2015/03/fanfiction-guide.html#essay.

2. Henry Jenkins, *Fans, Bloggers, and Gamers: Exploring Participatory Culture* (New York: New York University Press, 2006), 44.

3. Jenkins, 44.

4. Jenkins, 44–45.

5. Gabrielle Malcolm, "Introduction," in *Fan Phenomena: Jane Austen*, ed. Gabrielle Malcolm (Chicago: Intellect Books, 2015), 5–6.

6. Jenkins, 3.

7. Anne Jamison, *Fic* (Dallas: BenBella Books, 2013), 18–36.

8. Devoney Looser, *Jane Austen and the Discourses of Feminism* (New York: St. Martin's Press, 1995), 2.

9. Michael Thomas Ford, "The Jane Austen Vampire Trilogy," *michael thomasford* (blog), accessed February 23, 2018. http://www.michaelthomasford.com/jane-austen-series.html.

10. Jamison, 277.

11. Shannon Hale, "Our Friend Jane," *squeetusblog: official blog of shannon hale* (blog), http://www.squeetus.com/austen_friend.html.

12. See chapter 1.

13. tjmystic, "So, When I Was Doing My Thesis," *Let Not Your Hands Be Weak* (blog), Tumblr, accessed February 23, 2018. http://tjmystic.tumblr.com/post/141003600885/so-when-i-was-doing-my-thesis-on-whether-or-not.

14. Constance Grady, "Why We're Terrified of Fanfiction," Vox, June 2, 2016, https://www.vox.com/2016/6/2/11531406/why-were-terrified-fanfiction-teen-girls.

15. Affirmational fanfiction are works that conform to the established canon, meaning you will likely not see non-canon couples romantically paired, or find things like alternate endings.

16. Jamison, 19.

17. Catherine Tosenberger, "Mature Poets Steal: Children's Literature and the Unpublishability of Fanfiction," *Children's Literature Association Quarterly* 39, no. 1 (2014): 4–27.

18. Tosenberger, 8.

19. Longer, but not novel-length, stories usually unconnected to one another.

20. Any length, but usually indicating long reads, sometimes many chapters long, that describe an entire story.

21. Tosenberger, 7.

22. Tosenberger, 7.

23. Jamison, 284.

24. Bronwen Thomas, "What Is Fanfiction and Why Are People Saying Such Nice Things about It?," *Storyworlds: A Journal of Narrative Studies* 3, no. 1 (May 26, 2011), 8.

25. A "gift economy" means that creators are not paid for their work, or at least not monetarily. It works on the assumption that fans are creating and sharing out of love for the source material and fandom. Some fandoms will have "gift exchanges" where a writer might pen a story and exchange that with an artist for a painting, digital art, or another medium.

26. Jamison, 285.

27. Jessica Irene, "Reader Report: Pamela Aidan Signing at Third Place Books," *Austenblog* (blog), January 22, 2007, https://austenblog.com/2007/01/22/reader-report-pamela-aidan-signing-at-third-place-books/#more-1625.

28. Irene.

29. Sharon Lathan, "About Sharon Lathan," *Sharon Lathan, Novelist* (blog), April 27, 2011, https://sharonlathanauthor.com/about-sharon.

30. Lathan.

31. Sharon Lathan, "Novels," *Sharon Lathan, Novelist* (blog), July 13, 2017, https://sharonlathanauthor.com/novels.

32. Monica Flegal and Jenny Roth, "Writing a New Text: The Role of Cyberculture in Fanfiction Writers' Transition to 'Legitimate' Publishing," *Contemporary Women's Writing* 10, no. 2 (2016): 253–72.

33. Flegal and Roth, 265.

34. Constance Grady, "Fanfiction Isn't about Muting the Original Stories. It's about Heightening Them," Vox, June 6, 2016, http://www.vox.com/2016/6/6/11845000/fanfiction-difficult-stories.

35. All of these fanfictions actually exist, either online for free or published.

36. Crossover fic is where writers will blend two different worlds together, such as creating a story where Catherine Morland from *Northanger Abbey* meets the Doctor from *Dr. Who*. Some of them don't have to be so disparate, however. A story combining *Pride and Prejudice* with *Sense and Sensibility* could also be considered crossover fic.

37. Jamison, 10.

38. Ship wars happen when fans disagree about potential romantic interests for the characters. Fans will often identify themselves as a member of a team, such as "Team Darcy." Because it's the internet and we cannot all just get along, fans will sometimes have heated arguments over why they support one romantic partner over another.

39. Derbyshire Writers' Guild is one example where posting guidelines exist.

40. Jenkins, 43–44.

41. Jenkins, 50.

42. Stands for "one true pairing." An internet abbreviation for a romantic couple or pairing you love the most.

43. Not all fanfic plots follow the canon story, however, and some will pair non-canon characters together. In this case, we as readers of course do not know what the ending may bring.

44. Lev Grossman, "The Boy Who Lived Forever," *Time*, July 7, 2011. http://content.time.com/time/arts/article/0,8599,2081784,00.html.

45. Grossman.

46. Jamison, 35.

47. The laws governing US copyright are extremely complex and predate the internet, so we will not be discussing the intricacies in this text.

48. This practice is known as "filing off the serial numbers" in fanfiction circles.

49. Flegel and Roth, 259.

50. Flegel and Roth, 259–60.

51. Rachel Edidin, " 'Kindle Worlds' Lets Authors Publish Fan Fiction at Dubious Cost," *Wired*, May 23, 2013, https://www.wired.com/2013/05/kindle-worlds-fanfic-copyright.

52. Abigail De Kosnik, "Should Fan Fiction Be Free?," *Cinema Journal* 48, no. 4 (September 27, 2009): 118–24.

53. At least contemporary fans. Janeites were originally men, as discussed in the introduction.

54. Deborah Yaffe, *Among the Janeites* (New York: Houghton Mifflin Harcourt, 2013), xix.

55. Jamison, 19; also, Jenkins, 43.

CHAPTER 4

1. Bernie Su, *The Lizzie Bennet Diaries*, YouTube, 2012, https://www.youtube.com/channel/UCXfbQAimgtbk4RAUHtlAUww.

2. Video-blog, or a video diary; the word is a portmanteau of "video" and "blog." A video blog is usually seen on YouTube.

3. A shortened version of the word "adorable."

4. Bernie Su, *The Lydia Bennet*, 2012, https://www.youtube.com/channel/UCRt5wuVdwkFYvZdp7Bglhew.

5. Lori Halvorsen Zerne, "Ideology in 'The Lizzie Bennet Diaries,'" *Persuasions: The Jane Austen Journal* 34, no. 1 (2013), http://www.jasna.org/persuasions/on-line/vol34no1/zerne.html.

6. Zerne.

7. Alan H. Goldman, *Philosophy and the Novel* (Oxford: Oxford University Press, 2016), 116.

8. A common way to distinguish between different variations of characters in fan communities is to use the "*world*!character name" format. In this case, "*LBD*!Lydia" refers to how the character appears in the Pemberley Digital series, and we use "canon!Lydia" to refer to Austen's original depiction.

9. Goldman, *Philosophy and the Novel*.

10. Jane Austen, *Pride and Prejudice* (New York: Cambridge University Press, 2006), 301.

11. In *Lydia* episodes 17–19, Lydia learns that her mom has been paying Mary to tutor her, and Mary gets upset at Lydia for abandoning her to visit Jane in Los Angeles. The two tentatively agree to be friends, but Mary is not seen again in Lydia's vlogs.

12. Austen, 428–29.

13. Erin Wert, "Dear Lydia," *Erin's Mind* (blog), Tumblr, April 18, 2013, http://erinwert.tumblr.com/post/48276806167/dear-lydia.

14. John Mullan, Zoe Williams, Janet Todd, Lucy Mangan, Sebastian Faulks, Bharat Tandon, P. D. James, and Paula Byrne, "Jane Austen's *Pride and Prejudice* at 200: Looking Afresh at a Classic," *Guardian*, January 28, 2013, http://www.theguardian.com/books/2013/jan/26/pride-prejudice-200th-anniversary.

15. Lydia pushes away Lizzie after Lizzie's birthday gift and pushes away Mary, but in both cases there are underlying causes.

16. Hayley Adams, "Sex Tape Scandal Rocks Hank Green's 'The Lizzie Bennet Diaries,'" Hypable, January 31, 2013, https://www.hypable.com/sex-tape-scandal-rocks-the-the-liz zie-bennet-diaries.

17. Rebecca Tushnet, "'I'm a Lawyer, Not an Ethnographer, Jim': Textual Poachers and Fair Use," *Georgetown Law Faculty Publications and Other Works*, January 1, 2014, https://scholarship .law.georgetown.edu/facpub/1306.

18. Organization for Transformative Works, "Comments of the Organization for Trans- formative Works on U.S. National Telecommunications and Information Administration (NTIA) and the U.S. Patent and Trademark Office (PTO)," Public Comments on Copyright Policy Issues, October 2013, http://www.transformativeworks.org/legal/policy-comm ents-and-letters.

19. Transcript of Lydia's tweets:

That's the thing about people right? They want one thing an you're just, . . . Whatever. Like. What's the point? Ha. Hahhaha. F.

I can take care of myself. I don't need anybody. I DON'T. I don't. I don't,

I'm having the BEST new year. Stop telling me otherwise. Things are what you say they are right? Right ? Soyup. that.

Do what iwant. Fine. Good just me, and nothin wrong with what i do cuz hey my life effects ME so whagevsies I'm great.

20. Lydia brags about her relationship with Wickham in her letter to Mrs. Forster (Austen, 321), showing not only her happiness but her misunderstanding of her own situation.

21. These snippets of manipulation continue through the next few videos and are perhaps most present in "Special Two" (*Lydia* episode 28), in which Lydia and George, apparently having gotten back together after a fight, discuss their relationship and George makes sure to mention on camera that he loves her.

22. That of running away without marrying Wickham in the original *Pride and Prejudice* ver- sus having an abusive relationship that results in a sex video potentially being released on the internet.

23. Chloe Thompson, "Web Series Reworks Austen Characters," *Tartan*, March 31, 2013, https://thetartan.org/2013/4/1/pillbox/lizziebennet.

24. Thompson, 1.

25. Zerne.

26. Kaite Welsh, "The Best Vlog Reinventions of Classic Books," *Guardian*, January 12, 2015, http://www.theguardian.com/books/booksblog/2015/jan/12/vlog-classic-novels-zoella -jane-austen.

27. The Twitter and Tumblr accounts, though now dormant, are still available to peruse.

28. Examples can be seen in *LBD* episode 2, "My Sisters: Problematic to Practically Perfect," and *Lydia* episode 13, "Runaway."

29. Mullan et al., 5.

30. This worry is supported in the 1995 BBC adaptation, which depicts Lydia and Wickham living together in London, only one bed visible.

31. Zerne.

32. Our discussion of fanfiction, including stories written within the world of *The Lizzie Bennet Diaries*, can be found in chapter 3.

33. Kate Rorick and Rachel Kiley, *The Epic Adventures of Lydia Bennet: A Novel* (New York: Touchstone, 2015).

34. Rorick and Kiley.

CHAPTER 5

1. Christopher Hooton, "*Harry Potter and the Cursed Child*: JK Rowling Shuts Down Anyone with a Problem about Hermione Being Black on Twitter: 'Frizzy Hair Is Canon,'" *Independent*, December 21, 2015, https://www.independent.co.uk/arts-entertainment/theatre-dance/news/harry-potter-fans-delighted-that-black-the-cursed-child-actress-is-cast-as-hermione-in-series-all-a6781251.html.

2. Deborah Yaffe, *Among the Janeites* (New York: Houghton Mifflin Harcourt, 2013), xix.

3. Yaffe, 19–20.

4. As discussed in the introduction, the first "Janeites" were men.

5. Olivia Murphy, "Regency Lives Matter: Jane Austen So White? Not So Fast," ABC Australia, April 7, 2017, http://www.abc.net.au/religion/articles/2017/04/07/4650069.htm.

6. The mixed-race daughter of an English aristocrat, Belle was raised by her aristocratic father's family in eighteenth-century England. More: "Slavery and Justice Exhibition at Kenwood House," Historic England, accessed February 23, 2018, https://historicengland.org.uk/research/inclusive-heritage/the-slave-trade-and-abolition/slavery-and-justice-exhibition-at-kenwood-house.

7. Once the manservant of Samuel Johnson, he eventually became his heir, opened his own business, and married a local woman in England. More: Michael Bundock, *The Fortunes of Francis Barber: The True Story of the Jamaican Slave Who Became Samuel Johnson's Heir* (New Haven, CT: Yale University Press, 2015), 11–13.

8. *Lady Macbeth*, directed by William Oldroyd (2017; Northumberland, UK: Sixty Six Pictures, 2017), DVD.

9. Steve Rose, "*Lady Macbeth*: How One Film Took on Costume Drama's White-Only Rule," *Guardian*, April 15, 2017, https://www.theguardian.com/film/2017/apr/15/lady-macbeth-black-racial-diversity-british-costume-period-drama.

10. Henry Jenkins, *Fans, Bloggers, and Gamers* (New York: New York University Press, 2006), 40.

11. Jenkins, 54.

12. Gifsets: a set of .gif images put together to prove a point or make an argument, or sometimes just for looking at for fun. Fancasting: choosing models, actors, or other famous individuals that one would cast in a television or film adaptation of a text.

13. Jane Austen, *Mansfield Park* (New York: Cambridge University Press, 2005), 51.

14. macaroon22, "Now I Really Want a POC Version of Pride and Prejudice," *Colored Pencils and Caffeine* (blog), Tumblr, accessed February 23, 2018, http://macaroon22.tumblr.com/post/147910167191/now-i-really-want-a-poc-version-of-pride-and-.

15. valeriemperez, "Jane Austen Raceswap: Mansfield Park," Tumblr, accessed February 23, 2018. http://valeriemperez.tumblr.com/post/96489373268/jane-austen-raceswap-mansfield-park-gugu-mbatha.

16. lasocialista, "Dream Pride and Prejudice Cast," *Because Feminism* (blog), Tumblr, accessed February 23, 2018. http://lasocialista.tumblr.com/post/108979717385/dream-pride-prejudice-cast-so-far-so-i.

17. frogyell, "Modern Bennet Sisters," Tumblr, accessed February 23, 2018, http://frogyell.tumblr.com/post/144123362360/modern-bennet-sisters-for-the-pp-comic-order. Tumblr user frogyell has drawn comic book versions of the Bennet sisters and suggests that a full comic could be forthcoming, but as of this writing the link she provided on her post does not work.

18. Similarly to Austen, Rowling noted that the most defining characteristic that had been ascribed to Hermione in the books was brown, bushy hair. It is likely the casting of Emma Watson, a white woman, that led many pop culture fans to assume the character was written as white when in fact her race was not described at all.

19. Fanfiction is discussed in more detail in chapter 3.

20. Sarah J. McCarthey and Elizabeth Birr Moje, "Identity Matters," *Reading Research Quarterly* 37, no. 2 (April 6, 2002): 228–38, https://doi.org/10.1598/RRQ.37.2.6.

21. McCarthey and Moje, "Identity Matters," 235.

22. Elise Barker, "Playing with Jane Austen: Gender Identity and the Narrowing of Interpretation," Persuasions On-Line 31, no. 1 (2010), http://www.jasna.org/persuasions/on-line/vol31no1/barker.html?.

23. Barker.

24. See chapter 7.

25. Barker.

26. This account is a place for authors who are leaving AO3 to reassign their material. Some use it if they want to create a new account, others because they are leaving the site for some reason, and still others assign works there to protect their identity if they don't want to be associated with a certain fandom.

27. orphan_account, "Prejudice & Pride," Archive of Our Own, accessed January 4, 2018. https://archiveofourown.org/works/6128952/chapters/14045898.

28. This practice has a controversial place in fandom. There are strong merits to investigating the ways different binary genders are treated in various societies, but a lot of transgender fans are understandably uncomfortable with the term "gender swapped" and have voiced concerns and frustrations in various places in fandom that instead of using the phrase "gender swapped" or flipping binary genders it's a great place to introduce and represent the trans community instead. There isn't enough trans representation in media, or yet in fandom either, and hopefully this will change, including in situations and stories such as the one described here. There is also storytelling interest and merit in showing the different treatments of binary men and women in different eras and canon stories, although authors may want to be aware of the potential issues involved in cisgender swapping stories.

29. Mei Wei Lin, "Mr. Darcy's Vice," Archive of Our Own, accessed January 4, 2018, https://archiveofourown.org/works/12255210/chapters/27847992. This fic has since been deleted from AO3 and has been self-published (Mei Wei Lin, *Mr. Darcy's Vice*, self-published, Amazon Digital Services, 2018, Kindle, https://www.amazon.com/Mr-Darcys-Vice-Prejudice -Variation-ebook/dp/B07HDS2CFL).

30. See similar material in chapter seven.

31. Constance Grady, "Fanfiction Isn't about Muting the Original Stories. It's about Heightening Them," Vox, June 6, 2016, https://www.vox.com/2016/6/6/11845000/fanfiction-diffi cult-stories.

32. rosefox, "A Very Wentworth Christmas," Archive of Our Own, accessed January 5, 2018. https://archiveofourown.org/works/13065510.

33. lizcommotion, "A Question of Seduction," Archive of Our Own, November 25, 2015, accessed January 6, 2018, https://archiveofourown.org/works/8645470/chapters/19827574.

34. This is actually quite a common trope among *Pride and Prejudice* fan works, and those who ship Elizabeth and Charlotte as romantic partners can draw from canon evidence for

the two's relationship being something more than friendship. Charlotte Lucas, especially, is often read as a queer woman. More about this is discussed in chapter 7.

35. One can easily imagine Lady Catherine, for whom tradition and social standing is paramount, being ashamed of *both* aspects of her daughter's identity and hiding her away as "sickly," so that society has little opportunity to speculate about either.

36. Devoney Looser, *The Making of Jane Austen* (Baltimore, MD: Johns Hopkins University Press, 2017).

37. Barker, "Playing with Jane Austen."

38. Henry Jenkins, *Convergence Culture: Where Old and New Media Collide* (New York: New York University Press, 2008): 322.

39. Paul Booth, *Playing Fans: Negotiating Fandom and Media in the Digital Age* (Iowa City: University of Iowa Press): 9.

40. Bernie Su, *Welcome to Sanditon*, YouTube, 2014, http://www.youtube.com/playlist?list=PL_ePOdU-b3xeIJZtHVbO2rtSkoNp63bjR.

41. Pemberley Digital, "Domino, Start Recording," YouTube video.*Welcome to Sanditon*, May 23, 2013, https://www.youtube.com/watch?v=Mi19D-jN2kQ&index=5&list=PL_ePOdU-b3 xeIJZtHVbO2rtSkoNp63bjR.

42. Tim Glanfield, "Watch Out, the TV Fans Are Coming to Save Their Shows . . ." *Radio Times*, accessed June 5, 2018, https://www.radiotimes.com/news/tv/2018-05-23/watch-out-the -tv-fans-are-coming-to-save-their-shows.

43. John Jannarone, "When Twitter Fans Steer TV," *Wall Street Journal*, updated September 17, 2017, https://www.wsj.com/articles/SB10000872396390444772804577623444273016770.

44. Ricardo Lopez, "Ed Skrein's Bold Move to Opt Out of 'Hellboy' over Whitewatching Concerns Ratchets Up Pressure," *Variety*, September 5, 2017, http://variety.com/2017/film/ news/ed-skrein-hellboy-whitewashing-diversity-hollywood-1202545644.

CHAPTER 6

1. "Pride and Prejudice and Zombies: Reception," Wikipedia, accessed January 4, 2018, https://en.wikipedia.org/wiki/Pride_and_Prejudice_and_Zombies#Reception.

2. *Pride and Prejudice and Zombies*, directed by Burr Steers (2016; Buckinghamshire, UK: Cross Creek Pictures, 2016), DVD.

3. I am thinking, here, of similar comedy-horror films like *Warm Bodies*, *Zombieland*, and *Abraham Lincoln, Vampire Hunter* (another Grahame-Smith adaptation) that cropped up every few years in the 2010s.

4. Kevin McFarland, "Pride and Prejudice and Zombies Is one Braaaaaaainy Mashup," *Wired*, February 5, 2016, https://www.wired.com/2016/02/pride-prejudice-zombies-empowerment.

5. Alexandra Sourakov, "Pride and Prejudice and Zombies: A Feminist Manifesto," *Tech*, February 11, 2016, https://thetech.com/2016/02/11/zombies-v136-n3.

6. McFarland, "Pride and Prejudice and Zombies."

7. "Pride and Prejudice and Zombies Movie Reviews," Rotten Tomatoes, accessed February 23, 2018, https://www.rottentomatoes.com/m/pride_and_prejudice_and_zombies/reviews/?type=user.

8. metonymy, "The Mysteries of the Astronomy Tower," Archive of Our Own, December 24, 2015, https://archiveofourown.org/works/5512508.

9. fresne, "Northanger Abbey of Marin," Archive of Our Own, December 24, 2013, https://archiveofourown.org/works/1098669.

10. "Role-Playing Game," Wikipedia, accessed January 13, 2018, https://en.wikipedia.org/wiki/Role-playing_game.

11. HasEveryPenNameBeenTaken, "Jane Austen and Werewolves," Fanfiction.net, accessed January 27, 2018, https://www.fanfiction.net/s/6949895/1/Jane-Austen-and-werewolves.

CHAPTER 7

1. Juliet Mcmaster, "Sex and the Senses," *Persuasions: The Jane Austen Journal* 34 (2012): 42–56.

2. Deidre Lynch, *Janeites: Austen's Disciples and Devotees* (Princeton, NJ: Princeton University Press, 2000), 108–9, 164.

3. Devoney Looser, "Fifty Shades of Mr. Darcy: A Brief History of X-rated Jane Austen Adaptations," Salon, July 16, 2017, https://www.salon.com/2017/07/16/fifty-shades-of-mr-darcy-a-brief-history-of-x-rated-jane-austen-adaptations.

4. Jane's possible relationship with her sister would have been unlikely but is historically impossible in terms of lesbianism, which did not exist, and neither did recognized nonpenetrative lesbian or woman-loving-women sexual intercourse. Although we can now look back and identify women loving women as lesbians or other aspects of the LGBTQ+ spectrum, they would not have identified or been identified as such at that time. Danuta Kean, "Jane Austen's Lesbianism Is As Fictional As *Pride and Prejudice*," *Guardian*, May 31, 2017, sec. Books, http://www.theguardian.com/books/booksblog/2017/may/31/jane-austen-lesbian-fictional-as-pride-and-prejudice.

5. Thomas Day, "Sex and Sexuality in *Pride and Prejudice*," *The Use of English: The English Association Journal for Teachers of English* 67, no. 1 (Autumn 2015): 21.

6. Susan Korba, "'Improper and Dangerous Distinctions': Female Relationships and Erotic Domination in *Emma*," *Studies in the Novel* 29, no. 2 (1997): 140.

7. "One True Pairing," or a couple (or poly relationship) that a person wants to see more than any other.

8. "Femslash" is a woman/woman or female/female pairing. "Slash" is a male/male or man/man pairing, originated in the fanfiction of Kirk and Spock (of *Star Trek*). The pairing was written as Kirk/Spock, then K/S, and the slash separating the two names became the shortcut for the type of pairing in general.

9. penfairy, "I Didn't Know There Were Austen Gay Otps (I'm Very . . . ," *Mark My Worms* (blog), Tumblr, January 5, 2016, http://penfairy.tumblr.com/post/136606061369/i-didnt -know-there-were-austen-gay-otps-im-very.

10. Devoney Looser, "Queering the Work of Jane Austen Is Nothing New," *Atlantic*, July 21, 2017, https://www.theatlantic.com/entertainment/archive/2017/07/queering-the-work-of -jane-austen-is-nothing-new/533418/?utm_source=atltw.

11. Looser.

12. Charlotte Geater, "On Shipping: What's Disney's, What's Yours, and What's Mine," *Women Write About Comics*, December 7, 2015, http://womenwriteaboutcomics.com/2015/12/07 /52542.

13. "Shipping," or "relationshipping," is the expressed desire to see two or more characters in a relationship of some kind, such as a romantic pairing. Used as a noun and a verb, i.e., "Elizabeth and Darcy are my ship," or, "I ship Elizabeth and Darcy."

14. Geater.

15. Geater.

16. Usually seen in TV shows but it can occur in other media; "queerbaiting" is when writers hint repeatedly at a queer relationship but refuse to or sometimes are kept from making the relationship real, and instead the characters are revealed to be "actually straight."

17. "Bury Your Gays," TV Tropes, accessed November 5, 2017, http://tvtropes.org/pmwiki/ pmwiki.php/Main/BuryYourGays. "Bury Your Gays" is the trope that refuses to let LGBTQ+ characters have a happy ending and often kills off these characters to further other plot-lines, to offer respect without understanding the background of the community, or even to prove the point that all queer people are evil. There are many variations of this trope, including "Psycho Lesbians," "Too Good for This Sinful Earth," "Magical Queer," and "Depraved Homosexuals."

18. Deborah Yaffe, "The Austen Fiasco?," *Debora Yaffe* (blog), Moonfruit, April 16, 2015, http://deborahyaffe.moonfruit.com/blog/4586114521/The-Austen-Fiasco/9633997.

19. Deborah Yaffe, "Eligible: Skyline Chili and Marshmallow Fluff," *Deborah Yaffe* (blog), Moonfruit, May 9, 2016, http://deborahyaffe.moonfruit.com/blog/4586114521/Eligible-Skyline-chili-and-marshmallow-fluff/10703985.

20. Terry Pratchett, *The Truth* (repr., New York: HarperTorch, 2001).

21. Dened Rey Moreno, "I love that almost everyone I know, . . .'" Tweet, *@Hajabeg* (blog), August 10, 2017, https://twitter.com/Hajabeg/status/892934092085379072.

22. Sari Edelstein, "Pride and Prejudice and Transphobia," *Avidly* (blog), June 22, 2016, http://avidly.lareviewofbooks.org/2016/06/22/pride-and-prejudice-and-transphobia.

23. Edelstein.

24. Edelstein.

25. Curtis Sittenfeld, *Eligible: A Modern Retelling of Pride and Prejudice* (repr., Random House, 2016), 355.

26. Sittenfeld, 355.

27. Sittenfeld, *Eligible*, 356.

28. Lauren Thurman, "'I Ship It': Slash Writing as a Critical Tool in Media Fandom," honors thesis, University of Colorado Boulder, 2015), 42, http://scholar.colorado.edu/honr_theses/904.

29. Fanfiction in which the author inserts themselves into the story, often as a main character or love interest.

30. See, e.g., Kendra, "Confession Time: Why I Love Lost in Austen," *Frock Flicks* (blog), March 17, 2016, http://www.frockflicks.com/lost-in-austen-2008-2/; and lizzyandjane, "Lost in Austen and Fanfiction," *Theausteninheritance* (blog), May 4, 2012, https://theausteninheritance.wordpress.com/2012/05/24/lost-in-austen-and-fanfiction.

31. Eckart Voigts-Virchow, "Pride and Promiscuity and Zombies, or: Miss Austen Mashed Up in the Affinity Spaces Participatory Culture," in *Adaptation and Cultural Appropriation Literature, Film, and the Arts*, ed. Pascal Nicklas and Oliver Lindner, Spectrum Literature ser. 27 (Boston: De Gruyter, 2012), 43.

32. Camilla Nelson, "Jane Austen . . . Now with Ultraviolent Zombie Mayhem," *Adaptation* 6, no. 3 (December 2013): 339, https://doi.org/10.1093/adaptation/apt014.

33. "Suddenly Sexuality," TV Tropes, accessed December 29, 2017, http://tvtropes.org/pmwiki/pmwiki.php/Main/SuddenlySexuality.

34. "Sorry, I'm Gay," TV Tropes, accessed December 29, 2017, http://tvtropes.org/pmwiki/pmwiki.php/Main/SorryImGay.

35. Fan-made video often depicting the important moments between two characters that would indicate a potential relationship between them.

36. penfairy.

37. Sophie Lynne and Eleanor Thomas, *Interview: Devoney Looser*, podcast, 2017, https://soundcloud.com/the-bennet-edit/interview-devoney-looser: 47:38.

38. Michelle Hart, "The Queerness of Emma," *Book Riot*, July 18, 2017, https://bookriot.com/2017/07/18/the-queerness-of-emma.

39. Hart.

40. "An intelligent, hilarious & provocative voice and a progressively feminist online community for multiple generations of kickass lesbian, bisexual & otherwise inclined ladies (and their friends)," via Autostraddle's About page (https://www.autostraddle.com/about).

41. Cutting ties with someone (or a situation) by ceasing all communication and sometimes by standing someone up on a date.

42. Rachel, "Every Jane Austen Novel If They Were Gay and Also Historically Inaccurate," Autostraddle, June 10, 2016, https://www.autostraddle.com/every-jane-austen-novel-if-it-were-gay-and-also-historically-inaccurate-341322.

43. Rachel.

44. Heather Hogan, "10 Lesbian Sex Scenes I Wrote Before I Had Lesbian Sex," Autostraddle, September 8, 2015, https://www.autostraddle.com/10-lesbian-sex-scenes-i-wrote-before-i-had-lesbian-sex-306299.

45. Hogan.

46. Hogan.

47. Kean.

48. Simon Langton, "Pride and Prejudice," BBC America, 1995, Part 5, 36:41, https://www.amazon.com/Episode-1/dp/B00083IJKUW/ref=sr_1_2?s=movies-tv&ie=UTF8&qid=1519152562&sr=1-2&keywords=pride+and+prejudice.

49. *Pride & Prejudice*, directed by Joe Wright, Universal Studios, 2005. https://www.amazon.com/Pride-Prejudice-Keira-Knightley/dp/B000I9YLUI/ref=sr_1_3?s=movies-tv&ie=UTF8&qid=1519152562&sr=1-3&keywords=pride+and+prejudice, 1:12:39.

50. Fanfiction of a story whose canon is without explicit sex, written with sex scenes, often explicit.

51. Langton.

52. This is a really, really fantastic inside joke by the author. Currer Bell is the pseudonym for Charlotte Bronte. The common explanation is that Jane Eyre, the character, is based on what would have happened to Jane Fairfax of *Emma* had she not married and instead become a governess. Although that may be true, there is no actual evidence of this fact. Charlotte Bronte was not an adamant fan of Austen and wrote multiple letters to multiple recipients conveying her confusion at the praise heaped on Austen's works. She preferred *Emma* to *Sense and Sensibility* or *Pride and Prejudice*, however, so perhaps the stories are true! Bronte to Lewes, G.H., January 12, 1848, in *Selected Letters of Charlotte Bronte*, ed. Margaret Smith (Oxford: Oxford University Press, 2007), 98; Bronte to Williams, W.S., April 12, 1850, in Smith, *Selected Letters of Charlotte Bronte*, 161.

53. currerbell, "Pride and Prejudice Erotica," Archive of Our Own, July 4, 2016, http://archiveofourown.org/works/7385473/chapters/16775779.

54. currerbell.

55. Kate Beaton, "Austen Mania," in *Hark! A Vagrant* (Montréal: Drawn and Quarterly, 2011), 88.

56. Beaton, 88.

57. Defined by mithrandir in the *Urban Dictionary* (http://www.urbandictionary.com) as "the act of hanging around the object of your affections looking intense but never actually telling them how you feel. The term is named for Colin Firth who played Mr. Darcy in a film adaption [sic] of Pride and Prejudice and spent a lot of time 'firthing.' "

58. Kate Beaton, "Jane Austen Comics," Hark! A Vagrant (Webcomic), Tumblr, accessed January 7, 2018, http://www.harkavagrant.com/index.php?id=4.

59. Juliette Wells, *Everybody's Jane: Austen in the Popular Imagination* (London: Continuum International, 2011), 177, 181.

60. Linda Berdoll, *Mr. Darcy Takes a Wife: Pride and Prejudice Continues* (Naperville, IL: Sourcebooks Landmark, 2004), vii.

61. Ann Herendeen, "The Story behind *Pride/Prejudice*," in *Pride/Prejudice: A Novel of Mr. Darcy, Elizabeth Bennet, and Their Forbidden Lovers* (New York: Harper Paperbacks, 2010), 411.

62. Wells, 186.

63. Wells, 185.

64. Wells, 185.

65. Kathleen A. Flynn and Josh Katz, "The Word Choices That Explain Why Jane Austen Endures," *New York Times*, July 6, 2017, sec. The Upshot, https://www.nytimes.com/2017/07/06/upshot/the-word-choices-that-explain-why-jane-austen-endures.html.

66. Flynn and Katz.

67. Berdoll, 41.

CHAPTER 8

1. Charlotte Geater, "On Shipping: What's Disney's, What's Yours, and What's Mine," *Women Write About Comics*, December 7, 2015, http://womenwriteaboutcomics.com/2015/12/07/52542.

2. Danuta Kean, "Jane Austen's Lesbianism Is as Fictional as *Pride and Prejudice*," *Guardian*, May 31, 2017, sec. Books, http://www.theguardian.com/books/booksblog/2017/may/31/jane-austen-lesbian-fictional-as-pride-and-prejudice.

3. Vincent Chandler, " 'Love & Friendship' Review with Lisa Kennedy on 'Reaction Shot,' " *Denver Post*, June 3, 2016, https://www.denverpost.com/2016/06/03/love-friendship-review-with-lisa-kennedy-on-reaction-shot.

4. "Love & Friendship 2016," Movie Posters, Cinematerial, accessed July 14, 2018, https://www.cinematerial.com/movies/love-friendship-i3068194.

5. Whit Stillman, *Love & Friendship*, Streaming, Amazon, Amazon Studios, 2016, 5:16.

6. Stillman, 22:17–28.

7. "*Mean Girls* Quotes," Rotten Tomatoes, accessed July 15, 2018, https://www.rottentomatoes.com/m/mean_girls/quotes.

8. Jabba Wabba, *I Love You, Bitch*, Vine, YouTube video, December 24, 2014, https://www.you-tube.com/watch?v=0QoHrMPaLUs.

9. Stillman, 23:14.

10. Stillman, 56:20.

11. MercysBookishMusings, "Love & Friendship by Whit Stillman," YouTube video, June 1, 2016, https://www.youtube.com/watch?v=CTAKBObAqvY.

12. penfairy, "I Didn't Know There Were Austen Gay Otps (I'm Very . . . ", *Mark My Worms* (blog), Tumblr, January 5, 2016, http://penfairy.tumblr.com/post/136606061369/i-didnt-know-there-were-austen-gay-otps-im-very.

13. "Jane Austen + Text Posts," Tumblr, accessed July 21, 2018, http://janeaustentextposts.tumblr.com/post/145149944198; accessed July 26, 2018, http://janeaustentextposts.tumblr.com/tagged/Lady+Susan.

14. MercysBookishMusings, "Love & Friendship by Whit Stillman."

15. Stillman, 49:49.

16. Stillman, 36:50.

17. Stillman, 37:47.

18. Stillman, 1:19:54.

19. Stillman, 1:23:17.

CONCLUSION

1. Juliette Wells, *Everybody's Jane: Austen in the Popular Imagination* (London: Continuum International, 2011), 103–4.

2. Henry Jenkins, *Fans, Bloggers, and Gamers* (New York: New York University Press, 2006), 4.

3. Jenkins, 12.

4. Devony Looser, *The Making of Jane Austen* (Baltimore: Johns Hopkins University Press, 2017), 164.

Bibliography

AAMS. "A Happy Assembly." Review. *Meryton Playhouse*, June 1, 2016. http://meryton.com/aha/index.php?showforum=45.

Abad-Santos, Alex. "Kim Kardashian's Taylor Swift–Kanye West Snapchat Story, Explained." Vox. July 18, 2016. https://www.vox.com/2016/7/18/12210858/kim-kardashian-taylor-swift-snapchat-kanye-west.

"About Us." Republic of Pemberley. Accessed May 18, 2017. http://pemberley.com/?page_id=11874.

Adams, Hayley. "Sex Tape Scandal Rocks Hank Green's 'The Lizzie Bennet Diaries.'" Hypable. January 31, 2013. https://www.hypable.com/sex-tape-scandal-rocks-the-the-lizzie-bennet-diaries.

akika. "Second Attachments." Archive of Our Own. March 31, 2016. http://archiveofourown.org/works/4969153/chapters/11412064.

AMarguerite. "A Monstrous Regiment." Archive of Our Own, January 2, 2018. http://archiveofourown.org/works/10574634/chapters/23366709.

"Are the Shades of Pemberley to Be Thus Polluted?" Tumblr. Accessed February 24, 2017. http://halfagony-halfhope.tumblr.com/post/122544585196/darcy-and-elizabeth-second-proposal.

Austen, Jane. *Emma*. Edited by Richard Cronin and Dorothy McMillan. New York: Cambridge University Press, 2005.

———. *Mansfield Park*. Edited by John Wilshire. New York: Cambridge University Press, 2005.

———. *Northanger Abbey*. Edited by Barbara M. Benedict and Deirdre Le Faye. New York: Cambridge University Press, 2006.

———. *Persuasion*. Edited by Janet Todd and Antje Blank. New York: Cambridge University Press, 2006.

———. *Pride and Prejudice*. Edited by Pat Rogers. New York: Cambridge University Press, 2006.

———. *Sense and Sensibility*. Edited by Edward Copeland. New York: Cambridge University Press, 2006.

———. *Later Manuscripts*. Edited by Janet Todd and Linda Bree. New York: Cambridge University Press, 2008.

"AUSTEN Jane—Works." Archive of Our Own. Accessed November 12, 2017. http://archive ofourown.org/works?utf8=%E2%9C%93&commit=Sort+and+Filter&work_search%5B sort_column%5D=revised_at&work_search%5Bcategory_ids%5D%5B%5D=116&work_ search%5Bother_tag_names%5D=&work_earch%5Bquery%5D=&work_search%5Blan guage_id%5D=&work_search%5Bcomplete%5D=0&tag_id=AUSTEN+Jane+-+Works.

Barber, Nicholas. "Pride and Prejudice at 20: The Scene That Changed Everything." *Culture* (blog). BBC. September 22, 2015. http://www.bbc.com/culture/story/20150922-pride-and -prejudice-at-20-the-scene-that-changed-everything.

Barker, Elise. "Playing with Jane Austen: Gender Identity and the Narrowing of Interpretation." Persuasions On-Line 31, no. 1 (2010). http://www.jasna.org/persuasions/on-line/ vol31no1/barker.html?

Beaton, Kate. "Austen Mania." In *Hark! A Vagrant*, 87–88. Montréal: Drawn and Quarterly, 2011.

———. "Jane Austen Comics." Hark! A Vagrant. Tumblr. Accessed January 7, 2018. http:// www.harkavagrant.com/index.php?id=4.

"Beautiful Cinnamon Roll Too Good for This World, Too Pure." Onion. January 23, 2014. http://www.theonion.com/article/beautiful-cinnamon-roll-too-good-for-this-world -to-35038.

———. Know Your Meme. Accessed March 12, 2017. http://knowyourmeme.com/memes/ beautiful-cinnamon-roll-too-good-for-this-world-too-pure.

Benjamin, Jeff. "Why Iggy Azalea Recreated 'Clueless' for Her 'Fancy' Video." Fuse. Accessed February 5, 2018. https://www.fuse.tv/videos/2014/05/iggy-azalea-fancy-clueless -interview.

Bennett, Alanna. "Community Post: What A 'Racebent' Hermione Granger Really Represents." BuzzFeed Community. Accessed March 21, 2017. http://www.buzzfeed.com/alan nabennett/what-a-racebent-hermione-granger-really-represen-d2yp.

Berdoll, Linda. *Mr. Darcy Takes a Wife: Pride and Prejudice Continues*. Naperville, IL: Sourcebooks Landmark, 2004.

"Bing Lee and His 500 Teenage Prostitutes." *The Lizzie Bennet Diaries*. YouTube video. April 9, 2012. https://www.youtube.com/watch?v=2KjOskZJEAc.

Blankenship, Jessica, and Ella Cerón. "Present Day Clueless." Twitter. Accessed February 23, 2018. https://twitter.com/ModernClueless.

Booth, Paul. *Playing Fans: Negotiating Fandom and Media in the Digital Age.* Iowa City: University of Iowa Press. 2015.

"Breadsticks." Know Your Meme. Accessed March 12, 2017. http://knowyourmeme.com/memes/breadsticks.

"Breadsticks Meme." Tumblr. Accessed March 12, 2017. https://www.tumblr.com/search/breadsticks%20meme.

Brinton, Sybil. *Old Friends and New Fancies: An Imaginary Sequel to the Novels of Jane Austen.* Naperville, Ill: Sourcebooks Landmark, 2007.

Buenneke, Katie. "Why *Emma Approved* Didn't Work as Well as *The Lizzie Bennet Diaries* Did." *LA Weekly.* April 7, 2014. http://www.laweekly.com/arts/why-emma-approved-didnt-work-as-well-as-the-lizzie-bennet-diaries-did-4499200.

Bundock, Michael. *The Fortunes of Francis Barber: The True Story of the Jamaican Slave Who Became Samuel Johnson's Heir.* New Haven, CT: Yale University Press, 2015.

Bury, Liz. "Mr Darcy Surfaces as Statue in London Lake." *Guardian.* July 8, 2013. https://www.theguardian.com/books/2013/jul/08/mr-darcy-statue-pride-and-prejudice.

"Bury Your Gays." TV Tropes. Accessed November 5, 2017. http://tvtropes.org/pmwiki/pmwiki.php/Main/BuryYourGays.

Cartmell, Deborah. *Screen Adaptations: Jane Austen's Pride and Prejudice: A Close Study of the Relationship between Text and Film.* London: Methuen Drama, 2010.

Chan, Stephanie. "Kate Beckinsale's 'Love & Friendship' Wardrobe Brings Color to 18th Century Widow." *Hollywood Reporter.* Accessed July 21, 2018. https://www.hollywoodreporter.com/news/kate-beckinsale-chloe-sevigny-love-892514.

Chandler, Vincent. "'Love & Friendship' Review with Lisa Kennedy on 'Reaction Shot.'" *Denver Post.* June 3, 2016. https://www.denverpost.com/2016/06/03/love-friendship-review-with-lisa-kennedy-on-reaction-shot.

Chavez, Danette. "Chris Evans Won't Stop Fighting Real-Life Supervillain Donald Trump." *AV/News.* March 15, 2017. http://www.avclub.com/article/chris-evans-wont-stop-fighting-real-life-supervill-252129.

Clarke, Donald. "Love & Friendship Review: Fizzles with Wit, Intrigue and Creative Amorality." *Irish Times.* July 21, 2018. https://www.irishtimes.com/culture/film/love-friendship-review-fizzles-with-wit-intrigue-and-creative-amorality-1.2661800.

Clueless. Directed by Amy Heckerling. 1995. Los Angeles, CA: Paramount Pictures, 1999. DVD.

Crysty. "Contributor Guidelines **PLEASE READ BEFORE POSTING**." Derbyshire Writers Guild. June 23, 2008. Accessed May 18, 2017. https://www.dwiggie.com/phorum/read. php?5,2413,2413#msg-2413.

currerbell. "Pride and Prejudice Erotica." Archive of Our Own. July 4, 2016. http://archive ofourown.org/works/7385473/chapters/16775779.

Curzon. "Love & Friendship Q&A with Whit Stillman and Kate Beckinsale." YouTube video. June 10, 2016. https://www.youtube.com/watch?v=1YlaYDzDqUw.

Day, Thomas. "Sex and Sexuality in Pride and Prejudice." *The Use of English : The English Association Journal for Teachers of English* 67, no. 1 (Autumn 2015): 19–23.

Edelstein, Sari. "Pride and Prejudice and Transphobia." *Avidly* (blog). June 22, 2016. http:// avidly.lareviewofbooks.org/2016/06/22/pride-and-prejudice-and-transphobia.

Edidin, Rachel. " 'Kindle Worlds' Lets Authors Publish Fan Fiction At Dubious Cost." *Wired.* May 23, 2013. https://www.wired.com/2013/05/kindle-worlds-fanfic-copyright.

Eng, Matthew. "Kate Beckinsale and Chloë Sevigny's Bravura Comic . . ." Tumblr. Accessed June 26, 2018. http://tribeca.tumblr.com/post/156518058939/kate-beckinsale-and-chloë -sevignys-bravura-comic.

Erzen, Tanya. *Fanpire: The Twilight Saga and the Women Who Love It.* Boston: Beacon Press, 2012.

"Ever, Jane: The Virtual World of Jane Austen." MMORPG. Accessed February 19, 2018. http://www.everjane.com.

Fahy, Colette. "I Was Meant to Be Wearing Nothing." Mail Online. Updated January 23, 2015. http://www.dailymail.co.uk/tvshowbiz/article-2922738/Colin-Firth-says-meant -wearing-famous-Pride-Prejudice-lake-scene.html.

"FAQ." Pemberley Digital. Accessed January 29, 2017. http://www.pemberleydigital.com/ emma-approved/faq.

Flegel, Monica, and Jenny Roth. "Writing a New Text: The Role of Cyberculture in Fanfiction Writers' Transition to 'Legitimate' Publishing." *Contemporary Women's Writing* 10, no. 2 (July 1, 2016): 253–72. https://doi.org/10.1093/cww/vpw010.

Flynn, Kathleen A., and Josh Katz. "The Word Choices That Explain Why Jane Austen Endures." *New York Times*, July 6, 2017, sec. The Upshot. https://www.nytimes.com/2017/07/06/ upshot/the-word-choices-that-explain-why-jane-austen-endures.html.

Ford, Michael Thomas. "The Jane Austen Vampire Trilogy." *michael thomas ford* (blog). Accessed February 23, 2018. http://www.michaelthomasford.com/jane-austen-series.html.

fresne. "Northanger Abbey of Marin." Archive of Our Own. December 24, 2013. https://ar
chiveofourown.org/works/1098669.

Freytas-tamura, Kimiko De. "Mr. Darcy, You're No Colin Firth." *New York Times*. February 9,
2017. https://www.nytimes.com/2017/02/09/books/colin-firth-mr-darcy.html.

frogyell. "Modern Bennet Sisters . . . " *The Last Melon* (blog). Accessed February 23, 2018.
http://frogyell.tumblr.com/post/144123362360/modern-bennet-sisters-for-the-pp
-comic-order.

Geater, Charlotte. "On Shipping: What's Disney's, What's Yours, and What's Mine." *Women
Write About Comics* (blog). December 7, 2015. http://womenwriteaboutcomics.com/2015/12/
07/52542.

Glanfield, Tim. "Watch Out, the TV Fans Are Coming to Save Their Shows . . . " *Radio Times*.
Accessed June 5, 2018. https://www.radiotimes.com/news/tv/2018-05-23/watch-out-the-tv
-fans-are-coming-to-save-their-shows.

Goldman, Alan H. *Philosophy and the Novel*. Oxford: Oxford University Press, 2016.

Grady, Constance. "Why We're Terrified of Fanfiction." Vox. June 2, 2016. https://www.vox
.com/2016/6/2/11531406/why-were-terrified-fanfiction-teen-girls.

———. "Fanfiction Isn't about Muting the Original Stories. It's about Heightening Them."
Vox. June 6, 2016. https://www.vox.com/2016/6/6/11845000/fanfiction-difficult-stories.

Graham, Peter. " 'I Want to Be a Scavenger': A Conversation with Whit Stillman." Jane
Austen Society of North America, *Persuasions: The Jane Austen Journal* 38, no. 1 (Winter 2017).
http://jasna.org/publications/persuasions-online/vol38no1/graham.

Grossman, Lev. "The Boy Who Lived Forever." *Time*. July 7, 2011. http://content.time.com/
time/arts/article/0,8599,2081784,00.html.

Hale, Shannon. "Our Friend Jane." *squeetus: official blog of shannon hale* (blog). http://www
.squeetus.com/austen_friend.html.

Hart, Michelle. "The Queerness of Emma." *Book Riot*. July 18, 2017. https://bookriot.com/
2017/07/18/the-queerness-of-emma.

HasEveryPenNameBeenTaken. "Jane Austen and Werewolves." Fanfiction.net. https://
www.fanfiction.net/s/6949895/1/Jane-Austen-and-werewolves.

Herendeen, Ann. "The Story behind *Pride/Prejudice*. In *Pride/Prejudice: A Novel of Mr. Darcy, Elizabeth Bennet, and Their Forbidden Lovers*, 411. New York: Harper Paperbacks, 2010.

Hogan, Heather. "10 Lesbian Sex Scenes I Wrote Before I Had Lesbian Sex." Autostraddle.

September 8, 2015. https://www.autostraddle.com/10-lesbian-sex-scenes-i-wrote-before
-i-had-lesbian-sex-306299.

Hooton, Christopher. "*Harry Potter and The Cursed Child*: JK Rowling Shuts Down Anyone with a Problem about Hermione Being Black on Twitter: 'Frizzy Hair Is Canon' | The Independent." Independent. December 21, 2015. https://www.independent.co.uk/arts-enter tainment/theatre-dance/news/harry-potter-fans-delighted-that-black-the-cursed-child -actress-is-cast-as-hermione-in-series-all-a6781251.html.

invisibleicewands. "{Waiting Room}." Tumblr. Accessed June 26, 2018. http://invisibleice wands.tumblr.com/post/155540824474.

Irene, Jessica. "Reader Report: Pamela Aidan Signing at Third Place Books." *AustenBlog* (blog). January 22, 2007. https://austenblog.com/2007/01/22/reader-report-pamela-aidan -signing-at-third-place-books.

Jabba Wabba. "I Love You, Bitch." Vine. YouTube video. December 24, 2014. https://www .youtube.com/watch?v=0QoHrMPaLUs.

Jamison, Anne. *Fic: Why Fanfiction Is Taking Over the World*. Dallas, Texas: BenBella Books, 2013.

"Jane Austen in Popular Culture." Wikipedia. Last modified February 17, 2018. https://en .wikipedia.org/w/index.php?title=Jane_Austen_in_popular_culture&oldid=826076925.

Jane Austen Society of the United Kingdom. http://www.janeaustensoci.freeuk.com.

"Jane Austen + Text Posts." Tumblr. Accessed July 26, 2018. http://janeaustentextposts .tumblr.com/tagged/Lady+Susan.

"Jane Austen + Text Posts." Tumblr. Accessed July 21, 2018. http://janeaustentextposts .tumblr.com/post/145149944198.

"Jane Austen's 'Love & Friendship' Comes to Screen, and It's an Absolute Treat." NPR.org. Accessed February 5, 2018. https://www.npr.org/2016/05/13/477911585/jane-austens-love -friendship-comes-to-screen-and-its-an-absolute-treat.

Jannarone, John. "When Twitter Fans Steer TV." *Wall Street Journal*. Updated September 17, 2017. https://www.wsj.com/articles/SB10000872396390444772804577623444273016770.

JASNA (Jane Austen Society of North America). Accessed February 19, 2018. http://www .jasna.org.

Jeffers, Regina. "Austen Fandom vs. Austen Academics, a Guest Post from Melanie Rachel." *Austen Authors* (blog). November 19, 2017. https://austenauthors.net/austen-fandom -vs-austen-academics-a-guest-post-from-melanie-rachel.

Jenkins, Henry. *Fans, Bloggers, and Gamers: Exploring Participatory Culture.* New York: New York University Press, 2006.

———. *Textual Poachers: Television Fans and Participatory Culture.* 2nd ed. New York: Routledge, 2012.

———. "Acafandom and Beyond: Week Two, Part Two." Confessions of an Aca-Fan (ser). *Henry Jenkins* (blog). Accessed May 14, 2018. http://henryjenkins.org/blog/2011/06/acafan dom_and_beyond_week_two_1.html.

Johnson, Claudia L. *Jane Austen's Cults and Cultures.* Chicago: University of Chicago Press, 2012.

Kahler, KC. "KC in PA—Pride and Prejudice 2005 + Onion Headlines, Part . . ." Tumblr. Accessed March 12, 2017. http://kcinpa.tumblr.com/post/122885430458/pride-and-prejud ice-2005-onion-headlines-part.

———. "Austen + The Onion Masterpost." Tumblr. Accessed May 18, 2017. https://kcinpa .tumblr.com/post/129726481568/austen-the-onion-masterpost.

———. "KC in PA—Kcinpa: (Via Austen + Onion Headlines: . . ." Tumblr. Accessed May 18, 2017. https://kcinpa.tumblr.com/post/125781551483/kcinpa-via-austen-onion-headlines.

Kean, Danuta. "Jane Austen's Lesbianism Is As Fictional As *Pride and Prejudice.*" *Guardian*, May 31, 2017, sec. Books. http://www.theguardian.com/books/booksblog/2017/may/31/ jane-austen-lesbian-fictional-as-pride-and-prejudice.

Kendra. "Confession Time: Why I Love Lost in Austen." *Frock Flicks* (blog). March 17, 2016. http://www.frockflicks.com/lost-in-austen-2008-2.

Kessler, Anton. "'I've Been Cursed by Darcy,' Says Firth." *Daily Mail.* Accessed April 17, 2017. http://www.dailymail.co.uk/tvshowbiz/article-136939/Ive-cursed-Darcy-says-Firth.html.

———. "Telling Men on Dating Sites about How I'm Convinced Charlotte Lucas Is a Lesbi-an Is How I'm Spending My Night. #NoRegrets." Tweet. *@amitygardens* (blog). July 10, 2017. https://twitter.com/amitygardens/status/883148040579817472.

Korba, Susan. "'Improper and Dangerous Distinctions': Female Relationships and Erotic Domination in *Emma.*" *Studies in the Novel* 29, no. 2 (1997): 139–63.

Kosnik, Abigail De. "Should Fan Fiction Be Free?" *Cinema Journal* 48, no. 4 (September 27, 2009): 118–24. https://doi.org/10.1353/cj.0.0144.

Lady Macbeth. Directed by William Oldroyd. 2017. Northumberland, UK: Sixty Six Pictures, 2017. DVD.

"Lady Susan Facsimile." March 20, 2014. http://www.themorgan.org/collection/jane-aus ten/lady-susan.

Lang, Cady. "10 Convincing Theories about Taylor Swift's New Album." *Time*. September 27, 2017. http://time.com/4944028/taylor-swift-reputation-album-theories.

Langton, Simon. "Pride and Prejudice." BBC America. 1995. https://www.amazon.com/ Episode-1/dp/B00083IJKUW/ref=sr_1_2?s=movies-tv&ie=UTF8&qid=1519152562&sr=1-2&key words=pride+and+prejudice.

lasocialista. "Dream Pride & Prejudice Cast So Far." *Because Feminism* (blog). Tumblr. Accessed February 23, 2018. http://lasocialista.tumblr.com/post/108979717385/dream-pride -prejudice-cast-so-far-so-i.

Lathan, Sharon. "About Sharon Lathan." *Sharon Lathan, Novelist* (blog). April 27, 2011. https:// sharonlathanauthor.com/about-sharon.

———. "Novels." *Sharon Lathan, Novelist* (blog). July 13, 2017. https://sharonlathanauthor .com/novels.

Leszkiewicz, Anna. "Taylor Swift Leans in to Her Villainous Persona on Reputation." *New Statesman*. November 10, 2017. https://www.newstatesman.com/culture/music-theatre /2017/11/taylor-swift-reputation-new-album-villain-bad.

Lin, Mei Wei. "Mr. Darcy's Vice." Archive of Our Own. Accessed January 4, 2018. https:// archiveofourown.org/works/12255210/chapters/27847992. Site discontinued.

———. *Mr. Darcy's Vice*. Self-published. Amazon Digital Services, 2018. Kindle. https:// www.amazon.com/Mr-Darcys-Vice-Prejudice-Variation-ebook/dp/B07HDS2CFL.

lizcommotion. "A Question of Seduction." Archive of Our Own. November 25, 2016. Accessed January 6, 2018. https://archiveofourown.org/works/8645470?view_full_work=true.

lizzyandjane. "Lost in Austen and Fanfiction." *Theausteninheritance* (blog). May 4, 2012. https://theausteninheritance.wordpress.com/2012/05/24/lost-in-austen-and-fanfiction.

Looser, Devoney. *Jane Austen and the Discourses of Feminism*. New York: St. Martin's Press, 1995. https://www.salon.com/2017/07/16/fifty-shades-of-mr-darcy-a-brief-history-of-x-rated -jane-austen-adaptations.

———. *The Making of Jane Austen*. Baltimore: Johns Hopkins University Press, 2017.

———. "Fifty Shades of Mr. Darcy: A Brief History of X-rated Jane Austen Adaptations." Salon. July 16, 2017. https://www.salon.com/2017/07/16/fifty-shades-of-mr-darcy-a-brief -history-of-x-rated-jane-austen-adaptations.

———. "Queering the Work of Jane Austen Is Nothing New." *Atlantic*. July 21, 2017. https:// www.theatlantic.com/entertainment/archive/2017/07/queering-the-work-of-jane-austen -is-nothing-new/533418/?utm_source=atltw.

Lopez, Ricardo. "Ed Skrein's Bold Move to Opt Out of 'Hellboy' over Whitewashing Concerns Ratchets Up Pressure." *Variety*. September 5, 2017. http://variety.com/2017/film/news/ed-skrein-hellboy-whitewashing-diversity-hollywood-1202545644.

Love & Friendship production notes. Accessed February 5, 2018. https://curzonblob.blob.core.windows.net/media/5270/love-and-friendship-production-notes.pdf.

"Love & Friendship 2016." Movie Posters. Cinematerial. Accessed July 14, 2018. https://www.cinematerial.com/movies/love-friendship-i3068194.

Lynch, Deidre. *Janeites: Austen's Disciples and Devotees*. Princeton, NJ: Princeton University Press, 2000.

Lynne, Sophie, and Eleanor Thomas. *Interview: Devoney Looser*. Podcast, 2017. https://soundcloud.com/the-bennet-edit/interview-devoney-looser.

mithrandir. "Firthing." Urban Dictionary, August 27, 2013. http://www.urbandictionary.com/define.php?term=Firthing.

macaroon22. "Now I Really Want a Poc Version of Pride and Prejudice . . . ." *Colored Pencils and Caffeine* (blog). Tumblr. Accessed February 23, 2018. http://macaroon22.tumblr.com/post/147910167191/now-i-really-want-a-poc-version-of-pride-and.

Malcolm, Gabrielle. "Introduction." In *Fan Phenomena: Jane Austen*, edited by Gabrielle Malcolm, 5–9. Chicago: Intellect Books, 2015.

McCarthey, Sarah J., and Elizabeth Birr Moje. "Identity Matters." *Reading Research Quarterly* 37, no. 2 (April 6, 2002): 228–38. https://doi.org/10.1598/RRQ.37.2.6.

McFarland, Kevin. "Pride and Prejudice and Zombies Is One Braaaaaaainy Mashup." *Wired*. February 5, 2016. https://www.wired.com/2016/02/pride-prejudice-zombies-empowerment.

Mcmaster, Juliet. "Sex and the Senses." *Persuasions: The Jane Austen Journal* 34 (2012): 42–56.

"Me, on a Date." *Off with the Fairies* (blog). Tumblr. Accessed May 8, 2017. http://lovnlife.tumblr.com/post/125763112635/me-on-a-date-so-have-you-read-pride-and

"*Mean Girls* Quotes." Rotten Tomatoes. Accessed July 15, 2018. https://www.rottentomatoes.com/m/mean_girls/quotes.

MercysBookishMusings. "Love & Friendship by Whit Stillman." YouTube video. June 1, 2016. https://www.youtube.com/watch?v=CTAKBObAqvY.

metonymy. "The Mysteries of the Astronomy Tower." Archive of Our Own. December 24, 2015. https://archiveofourown.org/works/5512508.

Miller, Laura. "You Belong to Me: The Fanfiction Boom Is Reshaping the Power Dynamic between Creators and Consumers." *Vulture* (blog). *New York Magazine*. March 11, 2015. http://www.vulture.com/2015/03/fanfiction-guide.html.

Mirmohamadi, K. *The Digital Afterlives of Jane Austen: Janeites at the Keyboard*. New York: Palgrave Macmillan, 2014.

Moreno, Dened Rey. "I love that almost everyone I know, . . ."' *@Hajabeg* (blog). Tweet. August 10, 2017. https://twitter.com/Hajabeg/status/892934092085379072.

Mullan, John, Zoe Williams, Janet Todd, Lucy Mangan, Sebastian Faulks, Bharat Tandon, P. D. James, and Paula Byrne. "Jane Austen's *Pride and Prejudice* at 200: Looking Afresh at a Classic." *Guardian*, January 28, 2013. http://www.theguardian.com/books/2013/jan/26/pride-prejudice-200th-anniversary.

Murphy, Olivia. "Regency Lives Matter: Jane Austen So White? Not So Fast." ABC Australia. April 7, 2017. http://www.abc.net.au/religion/articles/2017/04/07/4650069.htm.

NautiBitz. "In Heat." Nocturnal Light. 2007. http://spikeluver.com/SpuffyRealm/viewstory.php?sid=28212. 2007.

Neill, Natalie. "Gothic Parody." In *Romantic Gothic: An Edinburgh Companion*, edited by Angela Wright and Dale Townshend, 185–204. Edinburgh: Edinburgh University Press, 2016. http://www.jstor.org.resources.library.brandeis.edu/stable/10.3366/j.ctt1bgzd5s.12.

Nelson, Camilla. "Jane Austen . . . Now with Ultraviolent Zombie Mayhem." *Adaptation* 6, no. 3 (December 2013): 338–54. https://doi.org/10.1093/adaptation/apt014.

Of Heroes and Heroines (blog). Tumblr. Accessed June 26, 2018. http://loveofromance.tumblr.com/post/173844997015/lady-susan-lady-susan-vernon.

Organization for Transformative Works. "Comments of the Organization for Transformative Works on U.S. National Telecommunications and Information Administration (NTIA) and the U.S. Patent and Trademark Office (PTO)." Public Comments on Copyright Policy Issues, October 2013. http://www.transformativeworks.org/legal/policy-comments-and-letters.

paintmegolden. "Dancing with Our Hands Tied." Tumblr. *Dancing with Our Hands Tied* (blog), May 30. http://paintmegolden.tumblr.com/post/161252842758/next-up-in-line-for-queer-jane-austen-adaptations.

Paquian, Ruben. "Old Taylor Swift Fans Denounce Her Current Pop Persona." *Daily Texan*, November 16, 2017. http://www.dailytexanonline.com/2017/11/16/old-taylor-swift-fans-denounce-her-current-pop-persona.

Pemberley Digital. "Domino, Start Recording." YouTube video.*Welcome to Sanditon*. May 23, 2013. https://www.youtube.com/watch?v=Mi19D-jN2kQ&index=5&list=PL_ePOdU-b3x elJZtHVbO2rtSkoNp63bjR.

penfairy. "I Didn't Know There Were Austen Gay Otps (I'm Very . . . ." *Mark My Worms* (blog). Tumblr. January 5, 2016. http://penfairy.tumblr.com/post/136606061369/i-didnt-know -there-were-austen-gay-otps-im-very.

Pratchett, Terry. *The Truth*. Reprint, New York: HarperTorch, 2001.

Pride and Prejudice. Drama, 1938. http://www.imdb.com/title/tt0414386.

Pride & Prejudice. Directed by Joe Wright. 2005. Universal Studios. https://www.amazon .com/Pride-Prejudice-Keira-Knightley/dp/B000I9YLUI/ref=sr_1_3?s=movies-tv&ie=UTF8 &qid=1519152562&sr=1-3&keywords=pride+and+prejudice.

Pride and Prejudice and Zombies. Directed by Burr Steers. 2016. Buckinghamshire, UK: Cross Creek Pictures, 2016. DVD.

"Pride and Prejudice and Zombies Movie Reviews." Rotten Tomatoes. February 23, 2018. https://www.rottentomatoes.com/m/pride_and_prejudice_and_zombies/reviews/? type=user.

"Pride and Prejudice and Zombies: Reception." Wikipedia. Accessed January 4, 2018. https://en.wikipedia.org/w/index.php?title=Pride_and_Prejudice_and_Zombies&old id=818627478.

"Pride and Prejudice/The Onion Headlines : Period Dramas." Tumblr. Accessed March 12, 2017. http://whatwouldelizabethbennetdo.tumblr.com/post/119094313870/pride-and -prejudicethe-onion-headlines.

Rachel. "Every Jane Austen Novel If They Were Gay and Also Historically Inaccurate." Auto- straddle. June 10, 2016. https://www.autostraddle.com/every-jane-austen-novel-if-it-were -gay-and-also-historically-inaccurate-341322.

Rampton, Martha. "Four Waves of Feminism." Pacific University Oregon, October 25, 2015. https://www.pacificu.edu/about/media/four-waves-feminism.

"The Real Mr Darcy—A Dramatic Re-Appraisal." *Pride and Prejudice*. Drama UKTV. February 9, 2017. http://drama.uktv.co.uk/pride-and-prejudice/article/real-mr-darcy-dramatic -re-appraisal.

Robey, Tim. "Love & Friendship Shows Just How Funny Jane Austen Can Be—Review." *Telegraph*, May 26, 2016. http://www.telegraph.co.uk/films/2016/05/26/love—friendship -shows-just-how-funny-jane-austen-can-be—-revie.

"Role-Playing Game." Wikipedia. Accessed January 13, 2018. https://en.wikipedia.org/w/index.php?title=Role-playing_game&oldid=820099181.

Romano, Aja. "Canon, Fanon, Shipping and More: A Glossary of the Tricky Terminology That Makes Up Fandom." Vox. June 7, 2016. http://www.vox.com/2016/6/7/11858680/fandom-glossary-fanfiction-explained.

———. "Edgar Allan Poe Is Uniting All Your 2016 Social Phobias in One Surprisingly Durable Meme." Vox. October 14, 2016. http://www.vox.com/2016/10/14/13274974/tumblr-cask-of-amontillado-meme.

Rorick, Kate, and Rachel Kiley. *The Epic Adventures of Lydia Bennet: A Novel*. New York: Touchstone, 2015.

Rose, Steve. "Lady Macbeth: How One Film Took on Costume Drama's Whites-Only Rule." *Guardian*. April 15, 2017. https://www.theguardian.com/film/2017/apr/15/lady-macbeth-black-racial-diversity-british-costume-period-drama.

ryfkah. "Catherine's Fairy-Tale." Archive of Our Own. December 26, 2010. http://archiveofourown.org/works/144571.

Schuessler, Jennifer. "Mr. Darcy's Shirt Is Coming to America." *New York Times*. March 8, 2016. https://www.nytimes.com/2016/03/09/arts/television/mr-darcys-shirt-is-coming-to-america.html.

Schulmiller, Eric. "'Shipping' and the Enduring Appeal of Rooting for Love." *Atlantic*. December 27, 2014. http://www.theatlantic.com/entertainment/archive/2014/12/shipping-and-the-enduring-appeal-of-rooting-for-love/383954.

Sense and Sponteneity. "Dear Mr Darcy." YouTube video. May 4, 2017. https://www.youtube.com/watch?v=ekVdhO7P4Nw.

Sheffield, Rob. "Taylor Swift '1989' Album Review." *Rolling Stone*. October 4, 2014. https://www.rollingstone.com/music/albumreviews/taylor-swift-1989-20141024.

Shifman, Limor. *Memes in Digital Culture*. Cambridge, MA: MIT Press, 2014.

Sittenfeld, Curtis. *Eligible: A Modern Retelling of Pride and Prejudice*. Reprint, Random House, 2016.

"Slavery and Justice Exhibition at Kenwood House." Historic England. Accessed February 23, 2018. https://historicengland.org.uk/research/inclusive-heritage/the-slave-trade-and-abolition/slavery-and-justice-exhibition-at-kenwood-house.

Smith, Kyle. "Harry Potter Plays a Farting Dead Man in New Movie." *New York Post* Entertainment. January 23, 2016. http://nypost.com/2016/01/23/harry-potter-plays-a-farting-dead-man-in-new-movie.

Smith, Margaret, ed. *Selected Letters of Charlotte Bronte*. Oxford: Oxford University Press, 2007.

"Sorry, I'm Gay." TV Tropes. Accessed December 29, 2017. http://tvtropes.org/pmwiki/pm wiki.php/Main/SorryImGay.

Sourakov, Alexandra. "Pride and Prejudice and Zombies: A Feminist Manifesto." *Tech*. February 11, 2016. https://thetech.com/2016/02/11/zombies-v136-n3.

"Spy Drama Star Is 'New Mr Darcy.'" BBC News Entertainment. June 14, 2005. http://news .bbc.co.uk/2/hi/entertainment/3797535.stm.

Stampler, Laura. "This Picture of Benedict Cumberbatch as Mr. Darcy Will Make the World a Better Place." *Time*. September 16, 2016. Accessed June 18, 2018. http://time. com/3386696/benedict-cumberbatch-mr-darcy.

Stanfill, Mel. "'They're Losers, but I Know Better': Intra-Fandom Stereotyping and the Normalization of the Fan Subject." *Critical Studies in Media Communication* 30, no. 2 (June 1, 2013): 117–34. https://doi.org/10.1080/15295036.2012.755053.

"Star Takes Pride in New Prejudice," BBC News Entertainment, September 5, 2005, http:// news.bbc.co.uk/2/hi/entertainment/4180324.stm.

Stillman, Whit. *Love & Friendship*. Streaming. Amazon Studios, 2016. https://www.amazon .com/dp/B01F4CBBXI.

Su, Bernie. *The Lizzie Bennet Diaries*. YouTube. 2012. https://www.youtube.com/channel/UCX fbQAimgtbk4RAUHtIAUww.

———.*The Lydia Bennet*. YouTube. 2012. https://www.youtube.com/channel/UCRt5wuVdw kFYvZdp7Bglhew.

———.*Welcome to Sanditon*. YouTube. 2014. http://www.youtube.com/playlist?list=PL_ePO dU-b3xeIJZtHVbO2rtSkoNp63bjR.

"Suddenly Sexuality." TV Tropes. Accessed December 29, 2017. http://tvtropes.org/pmwi ki/pmwiki.php/Main/SuddenlySexuality.

"Taylor Swift's Career Timeline: From 'Tim McGraw' to '1989.'" *Billboard*. November 4, 2014. https://www.billboard.com/photos/6221976/taylor-swift-career-timeline-photo-gallery.

"Taylor Swift Unveils Even Darker Persona With New Single 'Skullfucking Maggot Shit Boyfriend.'" Onion Entertainment. September 1, 2017. https://entertainment.theonion.com/ taylor-swift-unveils-even-darker-persona-with-new-singl-1819580257.

Thomas, Bronwen. "What Is Fanfiction and Why Are People Saying Such Nice Things about It?" *Storyworlds: A Journal of Narrative Studies* 3, no. 1 (May 26, 2011): 1–24.

Thompson, Chloe. "Web Series Reworks Austen Characters." *Tartan.* March 31, 2013. https: //thetartan.org/2013/4/1/pillbox/lizziebennet.

Thurman, Lauren. "'I Ship It': Slash Writing as a Critical Tool in Media Fandom." Honors thesis. University of Colorado Boulder, 2015. http://scholar.colorado.edu/honr_theses/ 904.

tjmystic. "So, When I Was Doing My Thesis . . ." *Let Not Your Hands Be Weak* (blog). Tumblr. Accessed February 23, 2018. http://tjmystic.tumblr.com/post/141003600885/so-when-i-was -doing-my-thesis-on-whether-or-not.

Tosenberger, Catherine. "Mature Poets Steal: Children's Literature and the Unpublishability of Fanfiction." *Children's Literature Association Quarterly* 39, no. 1 (2014): 4–27.

Tushnet, Rebecca. "'I'm a Lawyer, Not an Ethnographer, Jim': Textual Poachers and Fair Use." *Georgetown Law Faculty Publications and Other Works,* January 1, 2014. https://scholarship .law.georgetown.edu/facpub/1306.

valeriemperez. "Jane Austen Raceswap: Mansfield Park." *all the stories are true* (blog). Accessed February 23, 2018. http://valeriemperez.tumblr.com/post/96489373268/jane-aus ten-raceswap-mansfield-park-gugu-mbatha.

Voigts-Virchow, Eckart. "Pride and Promiscuity and Zombies, or: Miss Austen Mashed Up in the Affinity Spaces Participatory Culture." In *Adaptation and Cultural Appropriation Literature, Film, and the Arts,* edited by Pascal Nicklas and Oliver Lindner, 34–56. Spectrum Literature ser. 27. Boston: De Gruyter, 2012.

Wells, Juliette. *Everybody's Jane: Austen in the Popular Imagination.* London: Continuum International, 2011.

Welsh, Kaite. "The Best Vlog Reinventions of Classic Books." *Guardian,* January 12, 2015. http://www.theguardian.com/books/booksblog/2015/jan/12/vlog-classic-novels-zoella -jane-austen.

Wert, Erin. "Dear Lydia." *Erin's Mind* (blog). Tumblr. April 18, 2013. http://erinwert.tumblr .com/post/48276806167/dear-lydia.

"What Is Autostraddle?" Autostraddle. Accessed October 25, 2018. https://www.autostrad dle.com/about.

"Where Do Emma's Videos Exist in World?" Pemberley Digital. Accessed January 29, 2017. http://www.pemberleydigital.com/where-do-emmas-videos-exist-in-world.

"Why Jane Austen's 'Emma' Still Intrigues 200 Years Later." *Time.* Accessed February 13, 2018. http://time.com/4130612/jane-austen-emma-200th-anniversary.

Yaffe, Deborah. *Among the Janeites*. New York: Houghton Mifflin Harcourt, 2013.

———. "The Austen Fiasco?" *Deborah Yaffe* (blog). Moonfruit. April 16, 2015. http://debora hyaffe.moonfruit.com/blog/4586114521/The-Austen-Fiasco/9633997.

———. "Eligible: Skyline Chili and Marshmallow Fluff." *Deborah Yaffe* (blog). Moonfruit. May 9, 2016. http://deborahyaffe.moonfruit.com/blog/4586114521/Eligible-Skyline-chili -and-marshmallow-fluff/10703985.

"You May Enjoy This Photo of Benedict Cumberbatch Dressed As Mr. Darcy." *Vulture* (blog). *New York Magazine*. September 16, 2014. http://www.vulture.com/2014/09/benedict-cumber batch-dressed-as-mr-darcy.html.

Zerne, Lori Halvorsen. "Ideology in 'The Lizzie Bennet Diaries.'" *Persuasions: The Jane Austen Journal* 34, no. 1 (2013). http://www.jasna.org/persuasions/on-line/vol34no1/zerne.html.

Index